BASIC CIRCUS SKILLS

BASIC CIRCUS SKILLS

by Jack Wiley

STACKPOLE BOOKS

BASIC CIRCUS SKILLS

Copyright© 1974 by
Jack Wiley

Published by
STACKPOLE BOOKS
Cameron and Kelker Streets
Harrisburg, Pa. 17105

Printed in the U.S.A.

Library of Congress Cataloging in Publication Data

Wiley, Jack.
    Basic circus skills.

    SUMMARY: Instructions for developing seventeen basic
circus skills including unicycling, juggling, tightwire
artistry, and clowning.
    1. Acrobats and acrobatism. 2. Circus.
[1. Circus. 2. Acrobats and acrobatics] I. Title.
GV551.W54   791.3'4   74-8896
ISBN 0-8117-0190-5

CONTENTS

PREFACE

AND ACKNOWLEDGMENTS

This book is largely based on my experiences as a performer from the seventh to twelfth grades in the Fresno YMCA Gym Circus, then under the direction of William V. McAlister, as a competitive tumbler from the seventh grade to the end of college, and as a teacher of circus skills when I was a YMCA Physical Director.

There are many books about the circus, but little information about how to actually perform circus skills. This book is an attempt to remedy the situation.

The author shown performing his unicycle act in the Fresno YMCA Gym Circus in the 1950s.

    Perhaps the person who really made this book possible is William V. McAlister, who first got me interested in circus skills and then taught me most of what I know about them. Many others contributed to this book in one way or another. Bill Jenack (Jenack Cyclists), who has devoted many years to promoting and teaching circus skills, spent many hours going over the manuscript. His many suggestions greatly improved this book. Special thanks are also extended to Jim Smith (Hamilton Mini Circus), Warren C. Wood (Great Y Circus), Dr. Hartley Price (Gymkana), and Dr. and Mrs. Miles S. Rogers (Wonderwheels).

chapter 1

INTRODUCTION

Almost everyone at one time or another has the desire to perform circus skills. The problem is how to go about it. There has been a void in available information, and the little that has been published is in widely scattered sources. This book is an attempt to remedy the situation.

A number of different circus skills have been included. The requirements for mastering them vary widely. Some, such as hand balancing, require a high degree of strength; others, such as juggling and balancing objects, involve mainly skill and coordination. All of the skills covered will not, of course, be for everyone. But from the large selection there's almost certain to be one or more that will be of interest to almost everyone.

There are literally hundreds of different types of circus skills. In order to do justice to the ones included, care in their selection was necessary. The criterions were their suitability for the beginner and the degree to which they could be considered as basic. Safety was also an important consideration. This eliminated activities such as teeter board and slack wire. However, ones that are included form the basis for these more advanced skills.

What do circus skills have to offer? First of all, they are fun! Imagine, for example, the thrill of making a wide sweeping turn on a unicycle or of juggling three clubs in perfect control.

Second, there's a large fitness element in many circus activities. Because the activities are so much fun, fitness may well be a secondary reason for doing them; nonetheless, it's there as an important bonus.

Third, circus skills are fascinating and challenging for all ages, male or female, and all levels of skill. And the fascination and challenge goes on and on. There's always another skill that can be learned, or one that can be done better. This can mean the adventure of going beyond, on a unique journey toward perfection.

Fourth, some of the circus skills are good training for, and can be used in other activities. The rolling cylinder board and unicycling, for example, are ideal training for sports requiring balance and agility, such as skiing and skating. Tumbling and pyramids can be used in cheerleading.

Fifth, circus skills are ideal urban activities. With a crowded environment and the energy pinch, their popularity is increasing rapidly. Many of the activities require only a minimum of space and equipment. ment.

Sixth, circus skills are ideal social activities. They can, of course, be done alone, but sharing an activity is a good way to get to know other people.

Seventh, circus skills are a means to artistic and creative expression.

Eighth, circus skills are entertaining to others. Of course, one can do them for his own amusement, but many people enjoy showing their skills to others. This may mean showing the skills to friends, performing as an amateur in gym and stage shows, or even going on beyond the skills covered in this book and becoming a professional performer.

Ninth, there are competitions in some of the activities, such as trampoline, horizontal bar, vaulting, and unicycling. Many people have found these activities more suitable and meaningful than the typical school sports.

Tenth, circus skills afford a unique opportunity to design and build equipment. While this is not the primary purpose of this book, information has been included for getting started. For example, a person might want to go on from the basic circus bicycles shown and design and build original ones. One man has a thriving business, which started as a hobby, of building special bicycles and unicycles for circus and parade riding use.

Circus activities are at last coming into their own as hobby and recreational endeavors at the amateur level. A number of amateur circuses are now well established, and others are being formed. There are many amateur circus clubs and groups, and circus skills are now being taught in a number of schools, colleges, camps, and community and volunteer organization programs.

This book is the first comprehensive source of information on basic circus skills. In the following chapters the basics of a number of circus activities are covered, each leading up to the point where a basic amateur act can be performed. Also covered are mechanics, history, where to buy and how to make circus equipment, how to form a circus club, and how to organize, promote, and stage amateur circuses.

chapter 2

TRENDS IN
UNICYCLE AND CIRCUS
ENTERTAINMENT

Performing circus skills dates back to the beginning of recorded history. Skills such as keeping balance on tightropes and juggling are so old that it is a matter of conjecture as to when they originated. In an unbroken chain these skills have been passed from generation to generation. Of all the forms of entertainment devised by man, circus acts have been the most persistently popular.

However, if one considers a circus in the modern sense as being made up of elements such as the ring, ring acts, and clowns, then the circus did not develop until toward the end of the 18th century, for it was then that all of these components were brought together for the first time by Philip Astley in London. Astley put together a complete show, using skills that had developed over thousands of years. He is known as the Father of the Circus. His show proved so effective that many of his ideas have become circus tradition and are still in use today.

The circus is presently a popular form of entertainment in almost every part of the world. Through the years new acts have been added and more difficult and spectacular stunts performed. While some of the present-day performers are doing stunts never before accomplished, some of the greatest performers to date lived long ago. Some of the outstanding feats that have been accomplished are described in later chapters.

In recent years the professional circus in the United States has been somewhat on the decline, but it's a long ways from disappearing. Recent performances in the United States by the Russian National Circus and the Shenyang Acrobatic Troupe have done much to revive interest.

Until quite recently circus skills were generally passed down in a family from one generation to the next, and only rarely were circus skills attempted by anyone outside these acts. The situation is vastly changed today.

PROMINENT UNICYCLISTS

A growing number of amateurs are performing circus skills, and some of the best professional performers of today are from non-circus families. One of them is Steve McPeak.

Steve McPeak

In 1965 Steve McPeak, an agile 20-year-old freshman at Asbury College in Wilmore, Kentucky, was walking aimlessly across campus when he noticed a student riding a unicycle. Steve's interest increased considerably when the rider stopped to talk to a girl, rocking the unicycle back and forth in one place. Recalling the incident, Steve said, "It was so neat I couldn't believe it. Right then I decided to learn to ride a unicycle myself."

It happened that Steve was watching one of the three unicyclists on campus, and they wanted another collegiate to learn so that they would have a four-man act for the college circus.

With six inches of snow on the roadway, Steve first attempted to ride a standard three-foot unicycle. That first day he managed to stay up long enough to have his picture taken. A month later, when he performed in the college gym show, he rode a six-foot high, chain-driven unicycle. Already he had become the best unicycle rider on campus.

Although he had no idea what the current record was, Steve decided that he wanted to ride a taller unicycle than anyone had ever done before. Even when he heard that someone had ridden a 15-foot unicycle, he did not change his goal.

To make up for his late start and the fact that he was not born in a circus family, Steve practiced constantly, riding his unicycle from class to class and to his meals. In fact, he unicycled everywhere. On weekends he often worked out on unicycles at the gym. Sometimes he went for long unicycle rides in the hills with his three unicycle companions.

For summer vacation Steve returned to his home in Hoquiam, Washington, and started working his way upward. First he designed, built, and learned to ride a nine-foot chain-driven unicycle. Then he moved up to a 12-footer.

When he returned to Asbury College in the fall, he took the 12-foot unicycle along with him. In the college circus that spring he not only rode the 12-footer forward, but also rode it backwards and rocked it back and forth in one place.

Back in Hoquiam the next summer Steve built and mastered other unicycles. One was a 13-footer, just two feet shorter than the tallest unicycle that had ever been ridden. Another was a three-wheeled model in which two wheels drove the main motion wheel. Even more unique was one fitted with a framework to support his body upside down so that he could pedal with his hands. He also started riding unicycles on a seven-foot high tightwire. He removed the tire from a three-foot unicycle and, holding a long pole to help maintain balance, learned to ride it across the wire. Before long he moved up to a wire suspended 35 feet above the ground.

In September Steve transferred to Seattle Pacific College in Seattle, Washington. In October he finished building a 20-foot unicycle, which was five feet taller than any unicycle that had ever been ridden up to that time. In November he used a ladder connected to a tightwire for mounting the 20-foot unicycle. Then he pedaled away from the ladder, made a large circle, and returned to the ladder. The record was his.

The feat is even more remarkable when you consider that it was accomplished less than two years from the time when Steve had first tried a three-foot unicycle.

In February of 1967 Steve traveled to New York, where he appeared on *I've Got a Secret*. His secret was that he rode the tallest unicycle in the world, which the panel failed to guess. Steve then rode the 20-foot unicycle before the TV cameras.

After the spring semester Steve quit college to become a professional performer. At the time he did two acts—one on the ground, the other on a 35-foot high tightwire. His ground act included riding the tallest unicycle in the world. For a finale on the 35-foot high wire he rode a 10-foot unicycle across without a net below. The best anyone else had ever done was a six-foot unicycle, and that had been on a wire six feet above the ground. For over a year Steve performed with small circuses along the West Coast.

In 1968, as a publicity stunt, Steve unicycled from Chicago to Las Vegas, making most of the distance on a 13-foot unicycle. Several times, because of high winds, he was forced down to a three-foot unicycle. In all, the trip covered 2,311 miles and took six weeks and one day. He averaged over 53 miles a day. (The only longer unicycle ride up to that time was made by Walter Nilsson in 1933 when he rode from New York to San Francisco, a distance of over 3,000 miles, in 117 days on an eight-foot unicycle. This record was broken

(Courtesy, Steve McPeak)

Steve McPeak on 13-foot unicycle with his brother, John McPeak, on his shoulders spinning plates on sticks. Steve used this unicycle for most of his Chicago to Las Vegas ride.

in 1973 by Wally Watts of Edmonton, Alberta, Canada, when he rode 4,550 miles across Canada in three months and one day.)

For a time Steve performed at Circus Circus Casino in Las Vegas. The low ceiling limited him to doing a ground act, but he set up a 35-foot high tightwire on a ranch just outside of Las Vegas and continued riding unicycles on the wire.

It was on this wire that Steve performed his greatest feat up to that time. He had constructed a special 20-foot unicycle—equal in height to his tallest-ever-ridden-on-the-ground unicycle. Then on December 15, 1968, he rode it across the 35-foot high tightwire without a net below.

It seemed unlikely that Steve could do anything to top this, but on February 2, 1969, he did. In the parking lot behind Circus Circus Casino he climbed a ladder to a special platform. Then he mounted a 31-foot unicycle, which towered almost to the height of an Olympic 10-meter diving platform. Thirty feet away was a second platform. He hesitated, working the pedals back and forth, which in turn moved the wheel far below.

Then he pedaled away from the support. Those watching strained their necks to look upward at Steve pedaling at the top of the long unicycle frame. After what seemed a long time—actually it was about a 30-second ride—Steve reached the second platform. With this he had added eleven feet to his old world record for riding the tallest unicycle.

Steve rode the 31-footer a total of four times, all on that same day. The longest ride was 100 feet.

At the present time Steve is concentrating on his high-wire act and no longer performs on the ground. In fact, the 31-foot unicycle, the tallest ever ridden to date, is on display in the American Bicycle Hall of Fame in Richmondtown, Staten Island, New York. The unicycle is suspended in a horizontal position. There wasn't room to stand it up.

Steven's present high-wire act includes riding a 10-foot zig-zag unicycle, a tandem unicycle, and the 20-footer, as well as stilt walking.

It is interesting to note that amateur unicycle riders are presenting the most serious challenge to Steve's record for the tallest unicycle ridden on the ground. Floyd Crandall of the Pontiac Unicyclists in Pontiac, Michigan, has already worked his way up to a 20-foot unicycle. Floyd and several other amateur riders are looking upward to the record. And the question remains, "If someone breaks the record, will Steve attempt to go higher yet?"

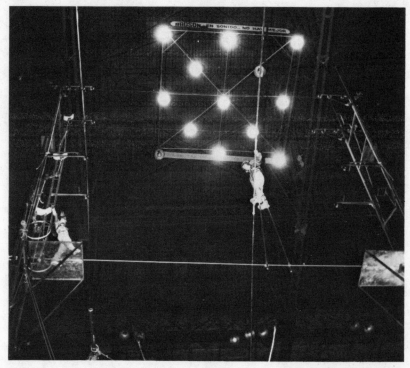

Steve McPeak recently added stilt walking to his high wire act. This photo was taken during a performance with the Atayde Circus in Mexico City.

Wonderwheels

The Rogers family of Cerritos, California, have been using cycling as the basis for a unique family venture. Known as the Wonderwheels, it started in 1964, first as a neighborhood unicycling group, then changed to a strictly family hobby at the end of 1968. The team now consists of Dr. Miles S. Rogers, a statistics professor and computer consultant who earned his Ph.D. at Princeton; Charlotte Fox Rogers, a former clinical psychologist with a master's degree from Northwestern; and their children, Craig, age 18; Dawn, 17; Bruce, 15; and Valerie, 13.

To date they have put on 148 costumed appearances, 87 of which have been competitive Southern California parades. They've won a sweepstakes trophy, a special award, 46 first place trophies, 18 seconds, and eight thirds.

The Wonderwheels performing a colorful unicycle routine.

AMATEUR CIRCUSES TODAY

Many schools, colleges, and community and volunteer organizations have put on amateur circuses. Some of these are held on an annual basis. Well-known groups include the Great Y Circus (Redlands, California), Circus Kingdom (Dover, Pennsylvania), Wenatchee Youth Circus (Wenatchee, Washington), Gymkana (Tallahassee, Florida), Sailor Circus (Sarasota, Florida), and the Hamilton Mini Circus (Hamilton, Ohio).

Fresno YMCA Gym Circus

During junior high school and high school in the 1950s, the author participated in the Fresno YMCA Gym Circus, then under the direction of William V. McAlister. The show was an annual event and featured a variety of acts, including tumbling, ladder pyramids, balancing, falling tables, unicycles, and trampoline.

Handbalancing act in Fresno YMCA Gym Circus in the 1950s.

Great Y Circus

The Great Y Circus in Redlands, California, evolved out of a "Family Night" back in 1929. Under the direction of Roy Coble, the event mushroomed rapidly into a real circus and, with the exception of the war years, has been held every year since. Roy Coble was circus director from 1929 to 1969; Dave Umbach directed the show in 1970;

Mrs. Ann Sackett and Warren Wood were co-directors in 1971 and 1972, and in 1973 Warren Wood was the director.

(*Courtesy, Warren C. Wood*)

Cradle act in Great Y Circus performance.

(*Courtesy, Warren C. Wood*)

In Great Y Circus performance Chuck Craw carries Lisa Floyd on shoulders while riding a unicycle.

The 36th annual production of the Great Y Circus (1974) is again under the direction of Warren Wood. Acts presently include webs, hanging perch, balance perch, roly-poly, bicycle pyramids, teeterboard, unicycling, clowns, rolling globes, trapeze, ladders, tumbling, tightwire, loop-the-loop, hand balancing, trampolining, juggling, and plate spinning.

At the present time none of the circus staff receives any pay—all donate time, talent, and money to help make the show possible.

Gymkana

The Florida State University Gymkana has gained considerable fame. Dr. Hartley Price started the group at the University of Illinois in 1935. When he took a position at Florida State University in 1947,

(*Courtesy, Dr. Hartley Price*)
Performing on the flying rings in the Florida State University Gymkana.

he continued the Gymkana there. Since then it has been held every year and has made special appearances in many parts of the United States.

Tallahassee Tumbling Tots

In 1949 Dr. Hartley Price organized the Tallahassee Tumbling Tots. The project grew to such proportions that in 1957 it was taken over by the City Recreation Department. The Tots participate in the Gymkana, including road trips. They have been featured in national magazines and have appeared in movies and TV shows, including the Mickey Mouse Club.

Sailor Circus

The Sailor Circus in Sarasota, Florida, currently involves over two hundred students, grades 2 through 12, from 21 county schools. It got its start in 1950 when Bill Rutland, a physical education teacher, included coeducational tumbling and acrobatics as part of a conditioning program. The group put on a demonstration and five hundred people crowded into a small gymnasium to see its premiere.

From this beginning the now internationally famous Sailor Circus

Tallahassee Tumbling Tots.

formed. In 1958 the show performed under a real circus tent, purchased with aid from the Booster Club.

Since its beginning in 1950, considerable attention has been focused on Sailor Circus. The show has been featured in movies and television programs and has performed not only in Sarasota but all over Florida, in other states, and even in some foreign countries. The Sailor Circus is currently under the direction of Bill Lee and held under 28,333 square feet of tented area accommodating more than 2,250 spectators each performance.

Besides performing, students are largely responsible for the work required to get ready for the performances, including raising the tent, painting, rigging, providing the music, and hundreds of other necessary jobs.

Hamilton Mini Circus

Just four years old, the Hamilton Mini Circus in Hamilton, Ohio, has grown from an original group of twenty boys and girls to over a hundred members ranging in age from eight to sixteen.

Since its first performance at a PTA meeting in January 1970, the Mini Circus has made over seventy appearances in Ohio, Tennessee, Kentucky, and Indiana. The Mini Circus features a variety of acts, including tumbling, acrobatics, unicycles, bicycles, trapeze, and teeter board.

One of the reasons for the success of the show is its dynamic director, Jim Smith. A graduate of Miami University in Oxford, Ohio, he has been teaching elementary physical education for twenty-two years. The last five have been at Lincoln Elementary School, home base of the Mini Circus. Mr. Smith is assisted by Carlos Looper, as well as a group known as the Sawdusters. The Sawdusters is made up of parents and friends of the Mini Circus performers. This group helps in transporting and rigging equipment, making costumes, spotting, and coaching some of the special acts. Also, they've sponsored a number of special projects to raise money to help support the show.

All of the many hours of work at practices, in shows, and on trips by the director, assistant director, and the Sawdusters is donated time. There are no paid Mini Circus personnel.

(Photo by Bob Lynn)

Pam Newkirk of the Hamilton Mini Circus performing on the single trapeze.

(Photo by Bob Lynn)

Seven performers on a bicycle. This is a popular act in the Hamilton Mini Circus.

chapter 3

SELECTING

CIRCUS SPECIALTIES

S ome of the circus activities will probably appeal to you more than others. A good starting point is to select an activity that you think you would enjoy or have always wanted to try.

GUIDE TO SELECTING ACTIVITIES

While most anyone who sincerely wants to can learn some of the basic skills for any of the activities included in this book, certain ones will probably be more appealing and suit the individual more than others. Also, in a few cases skills from another activity should be learned first.

Activities suitable for boys, girls, men, and women (anyone who wants to learn them with but few exceptions) are juggling, pole balancing, balancing a pole with spinning ball on top, balancing a stick with a spinning plate on top, diabolo, and many aspects of clowning.

Boys, girls, men, and women who have average levels of physical fitness can learn some or all of the basic skills in rolling cylinder board, stilts, tightwire, unicycling, bicycling, and some aspects of the ladders. However, the more difficult skills should be approached with discretion, especially by anyone beyond the college-age level. Children as young as five or six have learned skills in some of these activities with adult help.

Requiring a much higher level of physical fitness and therefore suitable for a more select group of boys, girls, and young men and women are tumbling, balancing, trampolining, rolled mat (mainly of interest to boys and girls up to about twelve years old), mini-trampoline, gym springboard, vaulting, horizontal bar, and trapeze. Older ages and those with lower levels of fitness have been successful at some of the skills in these activities, but extreme caution should be exercised.

Pyramids and ladders are suitable for boys, girls, men, and women of all levels of skill and physical fitness by selection of the parts to be performed. These activities are ideal in that both beginners and skilled performers can work together.

With some activities there are obvious conditions that preclude them from consideration. For example, a person who is overweight probably should not attempt tumbling. However, this same person might be successful as a bottom man in balancing (hand-to-hand, foot-to-foot, and so on).

In some cases skills from one activity are needed or helpful for learning another. Tumbling forms a sound basis for trampolining, rolled mat, mini-trampoline, gym springboard, vaulting, and for some aspects of clowning. It's recommended that unicycling be learned before attempting to ride a bicycle on one wheel. Tumbling and balancing can be learned together, as many of the techniques and skills are related. Since the horizontal bar is easier to spot than the trapeze, basic skills should be learned on the horizontal bar before attempting them on the trapeze.

Always try to select activities that are within your physical and mental capabilities, as some success is needed to sustain interest. Notice that some activities are primarily skill (juggling, diabolo, and balancing spinning plates on sticks). Others require high strength to body weight ratios, such as for tumbling and doing handstands. Activities such as unicycling and tightwire involve combinations of skill and physical factors.

APPROACHES TO LEARNING

There are many approaches to learning circus skills. With the instructions in this book it's possible to learn skills such as juggling and diabolo entirely alone. Others should never be practiced alone, but the person(s) with the learner need not necessarily be skilled at the activity. For some skills assistants and spotters are needed. It will often make things easier if at least two people learn together. This way they can alternate helping or spotting each other. The added element of seeing who can do a certain skill first will add to the fun.

Circus skills are also ideal for classes. A number of schools and colleges now offer circus skills classes. Some of the activities can be taught in follow-the-leader fashion. Vaulting, rolled mats, mini-trampoline, and gym springboard are particularly suited to this method, as the lines will move rapidly and there is little time to get bored. Others, such as juggling, unicycling, tightwire, and trapeze are best taught on an individual or small group basis. The skills covered in this book can be used so that each person can measure his own progress.

Circus skills classes should have as much activity as possible with a minimum of waiting for turns. Students will quickly lose interest if they have long waiting periods. Classes should be organized in such a way that everyone is practicing at more or less the same time. One or two short turns on a trampoline in a class period is a waste of everyone's time.

Classes can be formal or informal. Since formal methods have often been unproductive of interest in gymnastic classes, it's recommended that less formal methods be used.

Whether learning on your own or in a class, the artistic element is important. Most circus skills can be done with varying levels of skill. For performing in shows, each stunt needs to be sold.

CONDITIONING

In some cases conditioning programs are conducted before or along with learning basic circus skills. These programs are used to improve such factors as strength, flexibility, speed, and agility. Popular conditioning activities include jogging, running, calisthenics, and weight training. Many of the circus skills themselves include conditioning elements.

A conditioning program might follow each circus skills practice session. This might begin with some jogging. Chin ups, push ups, and sit ups might follow. A set routine will make it easier to stay with the program.

WARMING UP

In activities where the skill element is dominant, such as juggling, diabolo, unicycling, bicycling, stilt walking, pole balancing, and rolling cylinder board, the warm up can be the exercise of easy skills in the activity itself.

For activities calling for high levels of physical powers, a special warm-up should be used. It's recommended that the warm up be at least of fifteen minutes duration. A recommended sequence is:

1. Alternating jogging and walking with arm swinging for five minutes.

2. Stretching exercises, such as trunk flexion in straddle sitting position and back bends, for five minutes.

3. Calisthenics, such as side straddle hops and squat thrusts, for three minutes.

4. Finish with two minutes of light jogging.

TAPERING DOWN

After a vigorous circus activity workout, it's generally considered a good idea to taper down. What this amounts to is essentially doing exercise of gradually diminishing intensity. If conditioning exercises are done, the tapering down should follow them.

chapter 4

ALL ABOUT JUGGLING

Juggling balls, rings, clubs, and other objects is a fascinating circus skill. As a form of entertainment, juggling is hundreds of years old. Today there are many good professional jugglers. You've probably seen some of the best. They frequently perform with circuses and on the stage and appear on television.

At the present time Russia's Sergei Ignatov, one of the best jugglers in the world, has sometimes been able to juggle eleven rings, a world record, in practice. He estimates that it will be a couple of years before he will have it down to the point where he can use it in his act.

Juggling acts are popular in amateur circuses. By following the instructions in this chapter, you will be able to learn the fundamentals quickly.

EQUIPMENT

Although many objects, including plates, hats, bottles, knives, and flaming torches, can be juggled, our concern here will be with balls, rings, and clubs. However, after learning with these, you will be able to go on to more difficult articles, as the principles are the same.

Balls

All that you will need for learning the fundamentals of juggling are three solid rubber balls about two and one-half inches in diameter. Rings and clubs will not be needed until later, after the fundamental skills have been mastered with balls.

Balls suitable for learning to juggle can be purchased at variety and toy stores. Professional juggling balls are available from novelty shops, but these are more expensive and aren't really necessary for the beginner.

It may be helpful to have the three balls of different colors. Balls with a rough, unvarnished surface are best, as they are easier to handle. Also, if the balls have mold rings, use fine abrasive paper to remove them. This will make them more like the professional juggling balls, which are sold at a much higher price.

Rings

Juggling rings are easy to make from $\frac{3}{16}$- to $\frac{1}{4}$-inch sheets of plywood, fiberboard, plastic, or stiff cardboard. Cut the rings to the size shown. A coping or jig saw works well for this.

Depending on the material and its thickness, the weight of the rings will vary. There is no one weight that is best for everyone, so you may want to experiment with rings made from various materials until you find the ones that feel best.

For learning purposes, you will need three rings of the same size and weight. However, while you're at it, you may want to make more. Finish the rings by wrapping them with colored plastic tape.

Clubs

The juggling clubs used in professional acts may look heavy, but actually they are lightweight, either hollow or filled with a low-density core material. While there are a number of methods for making inexpensive juggling clubs, I feel that one of the best and easiest ways is to make them from toy plastic bowling pins, which can be purchased at variety and toy stores. Several sizes and colors are avail-

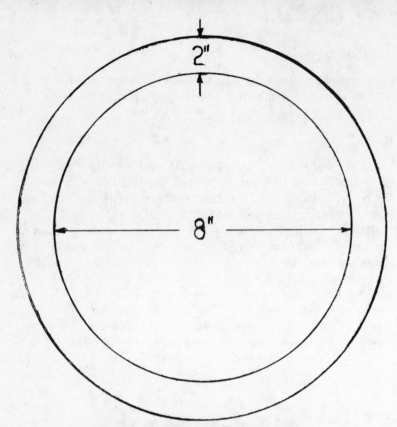

2"

8"

Pattern for juggling rings.

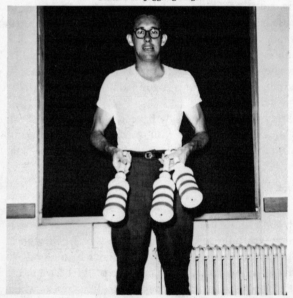

Juggling clubs can be made from the type of quart plastic bottles shown.

able. Ten-inch bowling pins were used for making the juggling clubs shown, but other sizes will also work.

Another good method is to make the clubs from quart plastic bottles of the type shown. Construction methods for bottles and bowling pins are similar.

Three clubs of the same size and weight will be enough to start with. However, while you're at it, you may want to make more.

Plastic bowling pins are made into juggling clubs by cutting (a hack saw works well for this) the pins into two sections at the narrowest point on the handles and adding a wooden dowel to the two sections of each pin, as shown. The doweling should be about ¾ inch in diameter. The handle from an old broom can be used, or you can purchase doweling at a hardware or lumber store.

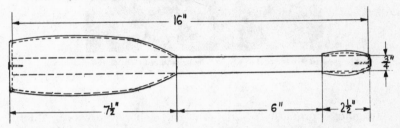

Pattern for making juggling clubs from 10-inch toy plastic bowling pins.

In order to fit the doweling into the bowling pins, it may be necessary to enlarge the holes in the necks of the pins. A round metal file can be used for this. To avoid splitting the dowels, drill pilot holes for the nails.

The exposed wooden parts of the handles can be wrapped with colored plastic tape. Also, if desired, circles of colored tape can be placed around the club bodies for decorative purposes.

Construction of juggling clubs from plastic bottles is the same, except that plastic or rubber chair-leg caps are used on the ends of the handles.

MECHANICS

Juggling is the art of keeping, if one hand is used, two or more objects in motion, alternately tossing and catching them and, if both hands are used, three or more objects. The main force acting on the objects being juggled is gravity. In some cases, especially with rings, air resistances are also a significant factor.

The exposed wooden part of handle is being wrapped with colored plastic tape.

Juggling is primarily a skill activity. Synchronized coordination is required and many hours of practice are necessary to achieve this. In time the tossing and catching patterns will become habit; it will no longer be necessary to think consciously about them.

When learning to juggle, it is important to learn the correct mechanics right from the start. Here are some important points to keep in mind:

1. A good toss in a predetermined flight path is required for a good catch.

2. In general, the objects juggled should be released at waist level and caught at chest level.

3. Look at the objects at the peak of their flight in the air. Do *not* watch your hands.

4. Relaxed wrists and quick tossing actions are recommended.

5. Juggling is best learned in a step-by-step manner. Practice each skill until it can be done with ease and control before going on to the next one.

6. If possible, practice at least fifteen minutes a day.

7. Some juggling skills require a starting hand. Use the hand that feels most natural to you. Right-handed jugglers generally use their right hands; if left-handed, their left. But not always. The illustrations

Look at the objects at the peak of their flight.

show the right hand as the starting hand from the point of view of the juggler, i.e., as though looking at your own hands. For showering, described later, the starting hand will determine the direction. If you prefer to use your left hand as a starting hand, you will need to reverse the directions shown for showering.

8. Learn all one-hand skills with both hands.

BASIC SKILLS

The two basic juggling patterns are cascading and showering. Cascading is a crisscross pattern; showering, circular. It is recommended that both patterns be learned with three balls before going on to rings.

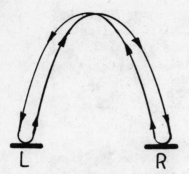
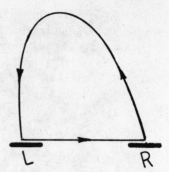

Cascading is a crisscross pattern.   **Showering is a circular pattern.**

In turn both patterns should be learned with rings before advancing to clubs, which are more difficult because they must be rotated in a prescribed manner. Regardless of whether you are practicing with balls, rings, or clubs, it is best to stand over a mattress or sofa. This will help to keep missed balls from rolling away. Since you'll be spending less time chasing them, you'll have more time for actual juggling practice. The padding will also help to prevent damage to rings and clubs when they are dropped.

If you drop one or more of the objects being juggled, pick them up and try again. On the more difficult skills you can expect many misses before consistent success. The old saying, "Practice makes perfect," applies particularly well to juggling.

LEARNING TO JUGGLE BALLS

One Ball and One Hand

Practice tossing the ball about two feet up. Catch it in the same hand that tossed it. Practice this until control can be maintained. The toss and catch should be made with the fingers rather than the palm of the hand.

Next try the same skill with the other hand. Again, practice until control can be maintained. Work for relaxed wrists and quick tossing actions.

One Ball and Two Hands

Toss the ball about two feet up in a slightly inward path and catch it in the other hand. After the catch has been made, quickly toss the ball about two feet up in a slightly inward path and catch it in the starting hand. Continue back and forth from hand to hand.

Again using one ball and both hands, try to vary the height of the tosses from one to three feet. Work for control. Remember to keep your eyes focused on the ball at the peak of the flight path. Do not look at your hands.

Two Balls and One Hand

After the above practice exercises have been mastered, it's time to try an actual juggling skill. Start with the hand that feels most natural to you. Hold both balls, one in the palm and the other at the finger tips. Toss the ball at the finger tips about two feet into the air and slightly inward. The other ball should be cupped in the palm of the

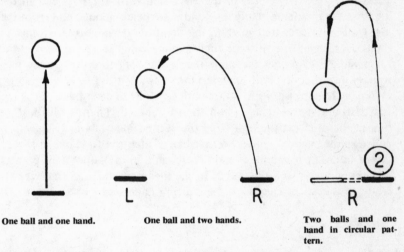

One ball and one hand.   One ball and two hands.   Two balls and one hand in circular pattern.

hand so that it is not released with the first ball. Allow the second ball to roll to the finger tips and quickly toss it into the same flight path as the first ball was tossed. Catch the first ball and toss it back into the air. Continue with this pattern. Notice that the balls are juggled in a circle. Finish by catching first one ball and then, without tossing the first ball caught, catch the second ball.

Next, learn the same pattern with the other hand. This will probably be more difficult, but it is important that this skill be mastered with each hand. Again, the circular pattern should be inward, i.e., counter-clockwise from the right hand and clockwise from the left hand.

A second pattern can now be attempted with two balls and one hand. Try the hand that feels most natural first. This time the flight path is straight up and down, with the second ball tossed inward and parallel to the first one. This skill is sometimes called the "fork" pattern.

This skill should then be learned with the other hand. Work for control and rhythm.

Before going on to the next skill, try all of the two balls and one hand juggling with different heights of tosses, such as one foot and three feet.

Two Balls and Two Hands

These are practice exercises that lead up to cascade juggling with three balls. Begin by holding one ball in each hand. Toss one ball straight up about two feet in the air. Then, with the first ball in the air, toss the ball from the other hand straight up about two feet in the air. Catch the first ball in the same hand as it was tossed from and then toss it again in the same flight path. Catch the second ball in the other hand and repeat the same toss again. Try to continue the pattern. Notice that one ball is always in the air.

The next exercise again starts with one ball in each hand. Toss the first ball about two feet up and slightly inward. Then, with the first ball in the air, toss the ball from the second hand about two feet up and slightly inward *under* the first ball. Catch the first ball that was tossed in the opposite hand and toss it again in the same flight path as used previously from this hand. In the meantime the ball that was already in the air is caught in the starting hand and tossed about two

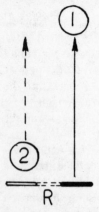

Two balls and one hand in "fork" pattern.

Two balls and two hands with each ball remaining on same side.

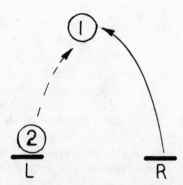

Two balls and two hands with balls switching sides.

feet up and slightly inward *under* the ball that is in the air. Try to continue the pattern.

Cascading with Three Balls and Two Hands

The cascade pattern is generally easier than showering. Thus, cascading should be learned first. Notice that the balls are tossed in a criss-cross pattern.

Begin by holding two balls in the starting hand and one ball in the other hand. Toss one of the balls from the starting hand about two feet up and slightly inward. Then toss the ball from the hand that had only one ball in it at the start about two feet up, slightly inward, and under the first ball that was tossed. Catch the first ball and at the same time toss the remaining ball from the starting hand. In each case, the ball should be tossed about two feet up, slightly inward, and under the ball that is in the air. Try to continue the pattern. If you drop one or more balls, pick them up and start again. A smooth finish can be made by not tossing one ball, catching a second ball in the same hand, and catching the other ball in the other hand.

It will probably take many hours of practice to learn cascade juggling with three balls to the point where the pattern is smooth and controlled and many rounds can be made without a miss. Timing is extremely important. Tossing a ball too soon or too late will make the pattern uneven and often results in a miss.

If serious difficulties are encountered in learning cascade juggling, it probably means that one or more of the fundamental steps were not learned well enough. If this seems to be the case, go back to the fundamentals and work up to cascading agin.

After cascading has been learned with the tosses about two feet up, try it with three feet and one foot heights. Also try varying the heights in the same juggling sequence. Then try cascade juggling with the hands close together and wide apart. Many combinations and variations will now be possible.

Two Balls and Two Hands

This is a lead-up exercise for showering. Begin with one ball in each hand. Toss the ball in the starting hand about two feet up in an inward path toward the other hand. Then, with the first ball in the air, toss the ball from the other hand *straight across* to the starting hand. Catch each ball in the opposite hands and continue the circular pattern. Practice this exercise until it can be done with control.

This exercise and showering with three balls can also be done in the opposite direction. However, since this is an advanced skill, you will probably want to wait until later before attempting it, after showering with three balls in the most natural direction has been mastered.

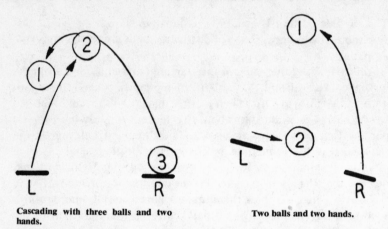

Cascading with three balls and two
hands.

Two balls and two hands.

Showering with Three Balls and Two Hands

Showering is juggling in a circular pattern. Begin by holding two balls in the starting hand and one ball in the other hand. From the starting hand toss the ball at the finger tips about two feet up in a slightly inward path toward the opposite hand. While the first ball is still in the air, toss the second ball from the starting hand in the same flight path as the first one. At the same time as the second ball is tossed, the ball in the hand that had one ball at the start should be tossed straight across toward the starting hand. Catch it and toss it upward and slightly inward in the same path as the first two balls, while at the same time catching the first ball that was tossed.

Continue tossing and catching the three balls in this circular pattern. At first, concentrate on making one complete round. Then work for two rounds, and so on. A neat finish can be made by not tossing two balls in sequence and catching the remaining one in one hand along with the ball that is already there.

Showering three balls depends a great deal on rhythm. With practice the pattern will become habit and it will not be necessary to think about it consciously.

After showering has been learned with the upward tosses about two feet into the air, try it with higher and lower heights. Also, you can change the heights during the same sequence.

The same procedure can be used for learning showering in the opposite circular direction. You may want to wait and come back to this later. It's more difficult than many of the skills detailed below.

Cascading Variation with Three Balls and Two Hands

Begin as in regular cascading. Use two different flight paths, one about half as high as the other. For example, the tosses from the right hand to the left can be two feet in the air; the ones from the left hand to the right, one foot up. Notice that in this case the tosses from the right hand are always over the ball coming from the left hand.

Many variations are possible. Switches can be made while juggling. For example, you can reverse the high and low tossing sides. Or you can alternate after each cycle with a one-over, one-under pattern.

Cascading Toss-out Pattern

This will add comedy to cascade juggling. While doing a low cascade pattern, toss one ball high and wide across to the other side. Reach out without looking in that direction and catch it at the last instant and continue with the cascade pattern.

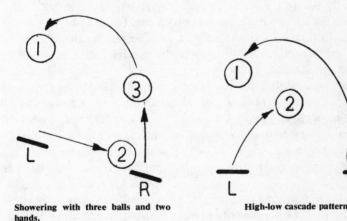

Showering with three balls and two hands.

High-low cascade pattern.

Switching Patterns

Switches can be made from showering to cascading, and vice versa. For example, begin with showering. Change to cascading by making the toss back to the starting hand upward and inward rather than straight across. A switch can be made back to showering again by going back to the straight across toss.

Further Variations

Here are some other variations of ball juggling. You may want to wait and come back to some of these later. At this point you're also ready to go on to ring juggling.

1. Juggle while walking forward and backwards.

2. Juggle while standing on a stool or chair. Also try stepping up from the floor to the stool or chair and then jumping back down while juggling.

3. Juggle while walking up and down stairs.

4. With regular juggling, toss one ball under leg and continue with regular pattern. This will probably be easiest with cascade juggling.

5. With regular juggling, toss one ball behind you and make the catch behind your back. Continue with the same pattern. Again, this will probably be easiest with cascade juggling.

6. While juggling, allow one ball to bounce off the floor. Continue with same pattern.

7. Same as number 6, except this time bounce the ball off a wall.

With a Partner

Begin by facing each other. Each juggler will use one hand. One juggler starts with two balls, the other with one. Begin by tossing one of the two balls upward and toward partner. The partner then tosses the one ball upward and toward partner, under the first ball. Continue with this cascade pattern.

Another basic skill is for one person to begin cascade juggling with three balls. The partner then moves in front of him and takes over with the cascade juggling. The switch should be made quickly and smoothly.

More difficult is to have partners stand side-by-side and both cascade juggle with three balls. On a called-out signal, each juggler makes a toss out toward the partner. Each juggler then continues with cascade juggling.

These basic partner skills form the basis for hundreds of possible combinations. It's also possible to work up stunts with three or more jugglers.

RINGS

Rings are generally tossed much higher than balls, so it's best to practice outside. After learning the fundamentals with balls, rings should not be difficult. All of the stunts described for balls except floor and wall bounces can also be done with rings. Follow the same progression for learning. Spin the rings as they are tossed.

Partner tricks with rings can be tried before going on to clubs, or you can come back to them later.

CLUBS

Juggling with clubs involves additional complications. Since the clubs must be caught with the handles across the fingers and palms of the hands, the rotation of the clubs in the air becomes important. Use a single rotation of the clubs at first. Later you can advance to two or more rotations. Use the center of the club handles for tossing and catching, not the knobs on the ends.

Using a single club rotation on each toss, follow the same progression as was used for learning cascade juggling with three balls.

Showering patterns with clubs are more difficult, as the tosses straight across with or without a rotation are difficult to execute. However, with practice they can be learned. Partner stunts can also be attempted at this time.

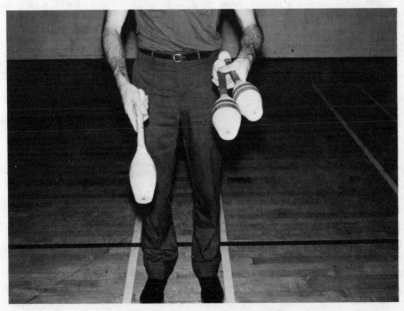

Starting position for juggling three clubs.

COMBINATIONS WITH BALLS, RINGS, AND CLUBS

After learning to juggle balls, rings, and clubs, try combinations, such as two balls and a ring or club; a ball and two rings; and a ball, ring, and club. The possibilities are numerous.

BASIC ACTS

From the juggling skills described above, you can work up an entertaining amateur act. Since hundreds of combinations are possible, and originality is important, the basic acts outlined are intended only as a guide to get you started. Here are a few general suggestions:

1. Use colorful costumes (see Chapter 22) and juggling equipment.
2. Good facial expressions are important. Practice in front of a mirror to make sure that you are not making faces or sticking your tongue out.
3. Make the act progressive by starting with easier tricks and gradually working up to more difficult ones.
4. Spend only a short time, generally ten seconds or less, on each trick before going on to the next one.
5. Between sequences, stop for applause and to catch your breath. Then go on to next sequence. Some professional acts are fast and almost continuous, but this requires a high degree of skill and a lot of endurance.
6. Comedy tricks mixed in with regular ones will make your act more entertaining. Complete comedy juggling acts are also possible, but difficult for most jugglers to do successfully.
7. A wheel cart can be used to hold juggling equipment.
8. Music and lighting can add to your act (see Chapter 22).

One Person

Only a skeleton is included. Be sure to work in any special tricks that you can do. However, make sure that they can be done consistently and well before adding them to the act.

1. Walk out onto the stage cascading three balls.
2. Do cascading variations.
3. Do cascading toss out. Pause.
4. Begin showering with three balls.
5. Do switches and combinations of showering and cascading. Pause after most difficult trick.
6. Do sequences with three rings. Stand sideways to the audience so that the surface of the rings will be in full view. Pause.

Juggling ball, club, and ring.

7. Do sequences with three clubs. Pause.

8. Do a sequence with a ball, ring, and club. Pause.

9. Finish with most difficult trick that can be done well. For example, a special up and down staircase can be used. Begin juggling, then walk up and down stairs.

How a professional performer handles the rings—Ken Benge.

With Partner

The same basic pattern can be used for acts with two or more jugglers, except that sequences of partner juggling should be added, including exchanges.

chapter 5

DEVELOPING BALANCING

AND SPINNING SKILLS

In this chapter a number of different circus skills are presented. Although any one of these could form the basis of an entire act, they are generally best used as part of another act or combined with one or more other skills. For example, balancing on a rolling cylinder board could be part of a unicycle act and juggling can be done while balanced on the board.

Skills such as diabolo have been used to form highly artistic acts. When the Shenyang Acrobatic Troupe toured the United States, many Americans saw diabolos for the first time, although this art is very old. However, such a high degree of skill is difficult to attain. For a beginner it would probably be best not to use this as the basis of an entire act.

The skills described in this chapter have one thing in common: they're all fun to try.

BALANCING A POLE

The equipment is simple. Round off the ends of an old broomstick and paint it a bright color or wrap decorative strips of plastic tape around it.

The basic principle used for balancing the pole is to continually move the base of support under the center of gravity. If the pole is being balanced in the palm of the hand, the eyes should focus at the top of the pole, not at the hand. If the pole begins to fall in one direction, the hand is moved in the same direction. By making a series of such corrections the pole can be kept in balance. Notice, however, that this is balance in motion. Stationary balance is rarely, if ever, achieved. Try, for example, keeping the pole in balance without moving the base of support.

Here are some basic pole balancing skills:

Palm of Hand

Hold pole in one hand and place lower end on palm of other hand. Release hold on pole and keep pole in balance by moving hand in di-

The basic principle used for balancing the pole is to move the base of support continually under the center of gravity.

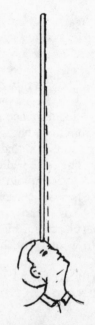

Balancing pole on forehead.

rection pole starts to fall. Remember to focus eyes on top of pole. With a little practice the required corrections will become automatic. All motions should be done calmly without hurried movements.

At first you may need to move around to keep pole in balance, but with practice this can be done while standing in one place.

Also try different arm positions, such as to side and up high and down low next to ground. Also try balancing pole with controlled walking. First try it forward, then sideways and backwards.

Index Finger

Next try balancing the pole on outstretched index finger. This should offer more control than balancing the pole on the palm of the hand. Again try different arm positions and controlled walking.

Back of Hand

This is a variation of the basic skill. The principles are the same.

On Chin

Next try the same balancing skills with the pole balanced on the chin. The eyes should focus on the top of the pole. Learn first without walking. Then try controlled walking, first forward, then sideways and backwards.

On Forehead

This one is a little more difficult, as the eye-pole relationship has been reversed and the eye-pole angle is slight. Again try first without walking, Then go on to controlled walking.

Variations

The above skills are only a few of the possibilities. Also try all hand and finger skills with the opposite hand. The pole can also be balanced on the tip of foot with leg extended. Then try kicking pole upward and catching it balanced in palm of hand.

Other variations include hopping pole in one hand while keeping it balanced and hopping pole back and forth from hand to hand. Or try balancing pole on palm of hand and then sit down, lie down on back, and return to feet again, keeping pole balanced. Another fun stunt is to walk up and down stairs while keeping pole balanced. This can be done with pole balanced on palm, finger, back of hand, chin, and forehead.

Slightly more difficult is to toss pole up so that it makes a half turn in the air and then catch it balanced on other hand. It's important to toss pole with just enough force to make it turn over by the time it reaches the level of the other hand.

BALANCING A POLE WITH
SPINNING BALL ON TOP

For this skill you will need to attach a disk to the end of a wooden pole about four feet long, as shown. The disk can be made of wood. It can be connected to the pole by using two small metal angle brackets. A rounded depression is carved in the top of the disk to present a slightly concave surface. A lightweight rubber ball about a foot to a foot and a half in diameter can be used.

The disk top can be painted black so that the rounded depression will not show. The pole can be painted a bright color or decorated with colorful strips of plastic tape.

The basic skill is to spin the ball on a finger, starting the spin with the same hand. The pole is held in the other hand just below the disk. Transfer the spinning ball to the depression on the disk. Then raise the pole and place the lower end in place for balancing. This can be on the palm, finger, or back of hand, chin, or forehead.

Most of the stunts with just a pole can also be done with the pole and spinning ball. If difficulty is encountered in keeping the ball balanced on the pole, the problem is probably that the depression is not properly shaped. Another common difficulty is in getting adequate spin on the ball. This may take a little practice. The action is to spin the ball quickly and catch it on a finger. It's usually easier with a light ball than with a heavy one, such as a basketball.

Balancing a pole and spinning ball makes an ideal addition to a juggling act. It can also be done while riding a unicycle or keeping balance on a rolling cylinder board.

BALANCING A STICK WITH
SPINNING PLATE ON TOP

This skill is much easier if a small round indentation is made in the exact center of the plate. A plastic plate can be used. A round stick about $5/16$ inch in diameter and three feet long is shaped to a point at one end. This will now fit the indentation in the center of the plate.

A 10- to 12-inch disk cut from ¼-inch thick untempered masonite

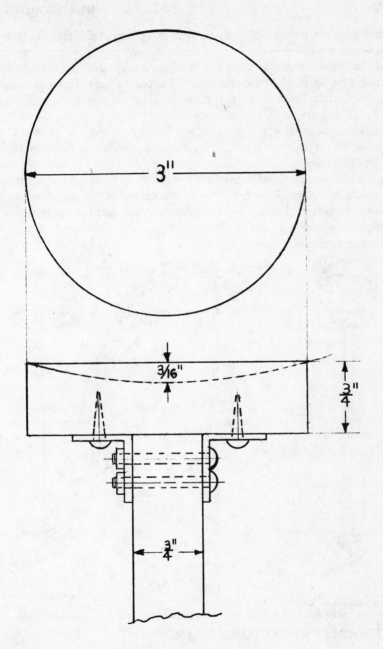

Disk attachment and construction.

can be used instead of a plate. Ball fringe can be added to give a colorful effect.

The basic skill is to start the plate spinning. Hold the stick in one hand and the plate in the other. Give the plate a spin. This may take a little practice. Once the plate is spinning, it should remain balanced easily.

After the basic plate spinning has been mastered, the stick can be balanced on various points such as palm, finger, or back of hand, chin, or forehead.

It should be pointed out that experienced plate spinners do not require the special indentation in the center of the bottom of the plate. However, theirs is a fairly advanced skill and their performance beyond the scope of this book.

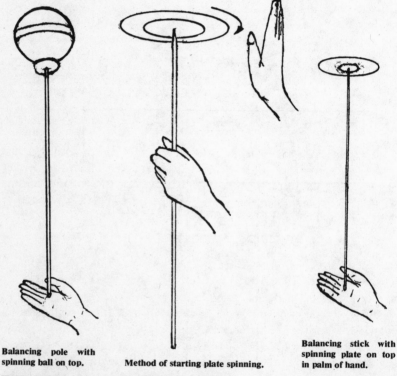

Balancing pole with
spinning ball on top.   Method of starting plate spinning.

Balancing stick with
spinning plate on top
in palm of hand.

THE ROLLING CYLINDER BOARD

This is fun and a challenging skill for all ages. Rolling cylinder boards are manufactured under various trade names and are available at sporting goods stores. Or you can construct your own, as shown.

In most cases a track is used to keep the cylinder in line and from going off at the ends of the board. The board can be used without this, but it's recommended for the beginner. Most of the manufactured boards have a track of this type.

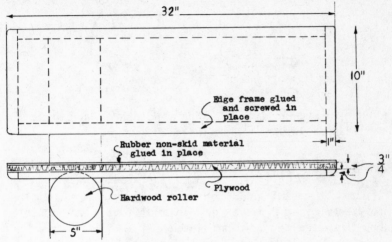

Plans for making rolling cylinder board.

Basic Balance

To start, position board on roller. Place foot on low end and step other foot to high end. Shift weight until both ends of board are free of ground. Try to maintain balance without having the board touch the floor. Try to maintain balance for at least a minute. Also practice shifting board back and forth without letting ends touch floor.

Parallel Stance

Start with basic balance. Then turn both feet toward one end of board and face body in that direction. Also try same skill with opposite foot forward. This position can be assumed by turning back to basic balance and then turning the other direction. Also try changing from one direction to the other with quick pivoting turn.

Squat Stance

Start with basic balance. Then bend knees to half squat position. Maintain balance. Also try full squat position. Another possibility is

Basic balance.   **Parallel stance.**

to alternate knee bends and standing while maintaining balance. Knee bends can also be done while in the parallel stance.

Side Stance with Feet Together

Start with basic balance. Shift to parallel stance. Gradually bring feet together until they are side by side. Balance is maintained over the roller by heel to toe shifting of weight.

Forward Stance with Feet Together

Start with basic balance. Gradually bring feet together until they are side by side over the roller. Use a slight knee bend and maintain balance by shifting weight.

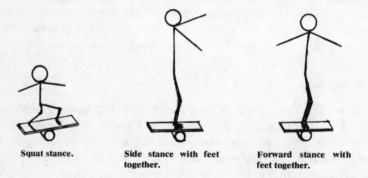

Squat stance.   **Side stance with feet together.**   **Forward stance with feet together.**

Jump

Start with basic balance. Jump a few inches off board with both feet and land again without losing balance. Gradually work up to higher jumps.

Jump with Half-Twist

This is a difficult one. Begin with basic balance. Jump with half turn and land on board facing opposite direction. This should be done without the board touching the ground.

Combining Basic Balance with Other Skills

If you have learned to juggle, try juggling skills while balanced on a rolling cylinder board. Other possibilities include balancing a pole, a pole with a spinning ball on top, and a stick with a spinning plate on top. Or try maintaining balance with a partner sitting on shoulders.

DIABOLO

The diabolo is fun and challenging. Diabolos can be purchased at toy stores. A set includes two sticks, a string (each end attached to the top of a stick) and a separate top, the latter of hourglass configuration.

Basic Spinning

Position the top over the string on the floor, as shown. Start the top rolling to left along the floor a few inches then lift the right hand quickly to accelerate it. Drop right hand slightly and lift it again quickly. Do this repeatedly until top gets up to speed. The left hand stick is just held in place with a rather loose grip that allows end of left stick to bob up and down just slightly to take up the slack each time the string is allowed to slip under the top on the down stroke of the right hand. Sticks are slowly returned to same level. Keep ends of sticks fairly close together and strings parallel. If top tilts toward you, correction is made by pushing right stick away. If top tilts away from you, correction is made by pulling right stick in.

It is important to remember that the diabolo top spins in only one direction. Lifting the left stick will slow rather than increase spin. Basic spinning should be practiced until it can be done easily and smoothly. The spinning action and balance corrections should become automatic so that you do not have to think about them.

Tossing and Catching Spinning Top

Begin with basic spinning. Make sure top is spinning fast and straight, then toss it into air by spreading sticks. Use right stick as a

Position of diabolo top over string on floor starting basic spinning.

Basic spinning.

Tossing spinning top.

guide for catching top on string. After top lands on string, quickly bring sticks close together to basic spinning position.

Bouncing Top on String

Begin as above, only this time spread sticks more slowly so that top is tossed only a few inches above string. With string tightly drawn, allow top to bounce on string several times before returning to basic spinning.

Uphill Climb

Begin with basic spinning. Increase top spinning to high speed. Lower right stock so that top is spinning near it. Straighten string by spreading sticks so that right stick is lower than left one. Top will now climb uphill.

Roll and Jump

Begin with basic spinning. Spread sticks by pulling outward with right stick. Top will jump to left. With tight string top will roll back to right. Toss top back to left again. Try to continue pattern as many times as possible.

Other Diabolo Skills

The above skills are only a few of the possibilities. It's also possible to catch the spinning top on the sticks. With a partner a top can be tossed from one string to another or can roll down two strings held end to end.

chapter 6

FUN ON STILTS

S tiltwalkers appear in the ancient folklore of many parts of the world, including China, Africa, and America. Stilts were used by traveling bands of entertainers in ancient towns along the Mediterranean Sea. Today, nearly every circus has one or more clowns on stilts.

The longest recorded journey on stilts was made by Silvain Dornon in 1891. He is purported to have walked from Les Landes, France, to Moscow, a distance of over two thousand miles, in 58 days.

Harry Yelding, a circus performer who lives in London, claims the world's record for walking on the tallest stilts. They measure 22 feet from his feet to the ground. When walking on these stilts, he is able to see in third-story windows.

Stiltwalking is fun to learn and popular for both regular and clown acts in amateur circuses.

EQUIPMENT

Stilts can be bought in toy and sporting goods stores, or you can make your own. Plans are shown for both hand-held and strap-on models. Hand-held stilts can be with or without foot straps. Those without the straps are recommended for the beginner. A good starting height is to have the footrests about a foot from the ground. The length of the handles will vary, depending on how the performer wishes to hold the stilts. If the stilts are to be gripped at the top, they should be about elbow height when the performer is standing on the footrests. The other method is to grip the stilts at hip level, with the handles of the stilts extending up behind each shoulder. These can extend above head height, making it possible to have adjustable foot rests by drilling additional holes.

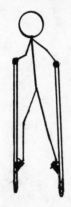

Elbow height stilts.

Hip level grip with stilt handles extending behind shoulders.

Strap-on stilts should be custom-made for the person who is going to use them.

A stair platform, as shown, can be used for stilt walking, as well as with other skills shown in this book.

MECHANICS

Maintaining balance on stilts involves keeping the center of gravity over the points of contact of the stilts with the ground. However, in practice this stationary balance is seldom achieved. Balance is generally maintained by a series of corrections. The contact points of the stilts with the ground are moved under the center of gravity. The mechanics are basically the same as in ordinary walking.

BASIC SKILLS

Begin with stilts with the footrests about a foot from the ground. It is safest to start without foot straps, as these can trap an ankle if the

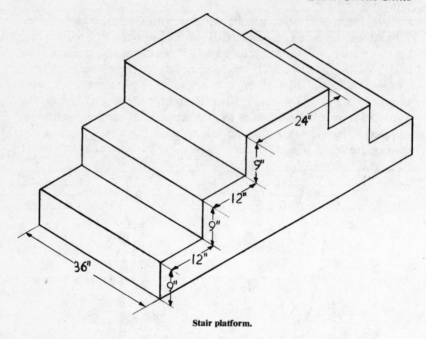

Stair platform.

learner starts to fall. After fundamental walking has been learned, foot straps can be added. These will hold your feet to the footrests, permitting you to raise the stilts with your feet as you walk. After the skills have been learned with one height, you can gradually work up to taller stilts. The basic skills should be thoroughly mastered with hand-held stilts before attempting them with strapped-on ones. The same learning progression can be followed.

Mounting

With the footrests close to the ground, it should be possible to mount the stilts in the open. Or you can use a stool or ladder. For taller stilts and strapped-on ones, a starting platform will be needed.

Fundamental Walking

Mounted on the stilts, lean slightly forward and start walking slowly forward. Look at the ground at a point some distance ahead, rather than directly below. Try to maintain control of the stilts. Remember, balance is maintained by walking in the direction of the lean. The upper body should remain upright.

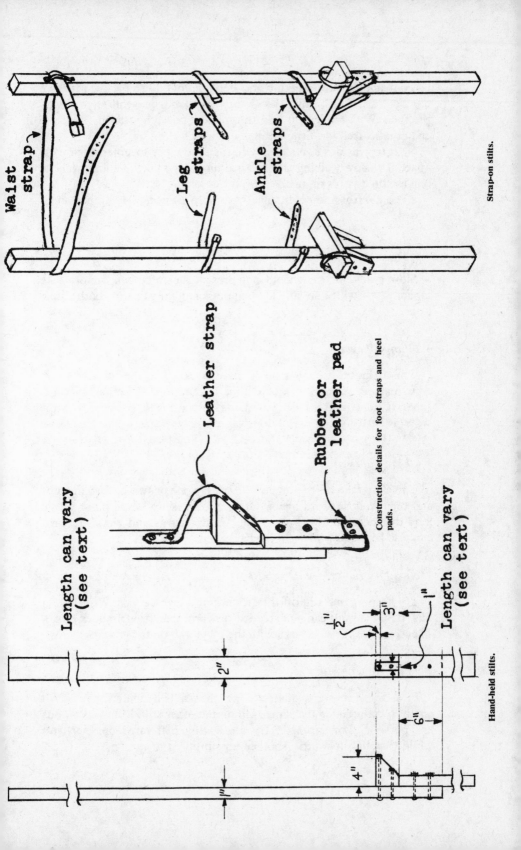

Waist strap

Leg straps

Ankle straps

Strap-on stilts.

Leather strap

Rubber or leather pad

Construction details for foot straps and heel pads.

Length can vary (see text)

2"

$\frac{1}{2}$"

3"

1"

Length can vary (see text)

Hand-held stilts.

6"

4"

1"

To dismount, stop walking and step one foot down backwards from the footrest. With low stilts, this shouldn't present any special problem. With taller stilts and strapped-on ones, the starting platform can also be used for dismounting.

Next try various size steps, with the stilts close together, then wide apart. Try slow walking and fast walking. Try to make a long walk of one hundred yards or more.

After control and confidence have been gained, foot straps can be added.

Turns

Slow gradual turns should not present any problem. Simply take longer steps with one stilt than the other. Learn to turn both directions.

Walking Sideways

This is more difficult than forward walking, as the forward-backward balance is more difficult. Practice first one direction, then the other. Circle patterns can be made forward and backwards while walking sideways.

Walking Backwards

This may take a little practice. First try one or two backward steps and then walk forward again. Gradually work up to the point where long distances can be walked backwards. Turns and circle patterns can also be made while walking backwards.

Momentary Balance on One Stilt

Try keeping one stilt off the ground for a few seconds. While doing this, the other stilt can be extended forward, then brought back down. Then practice the same skill with the other stilt on the ground.

Pivoting on One Stilt

First try pivoting a quarter turn, then a half, and finally a full circle. Next practice the same skill on the other stilt. Many variations are possible. For example, try alternating half turns on each stilt while traveling forward. Another possibility is to use one stilt like a scooter, while pivoting on the other one. Making a number of turns on first one, then the other stilt, makes an interesting combination.

Hopping on Two Stilts

Try hopping along on both stilts, first forward, then sideways and backwards. The main difficulty is in controlling the stilts.

Hopping on One Stilt

Try hopping on one stilt, with the other one off the ground. Then learn the same skill on the other stilt. Try combinations, such as alternating three hops first on one stilt, then the other one.

Obstacle Courses

Set up an obstacle course of automobile tires. Then go through the course on stilts, stepping only in the centers of the tires. Or walk across a 2- x 12-inch plank. To make this more difficult, set the plank on six-inch blocks. A plank with special stands can be constructed for use in shows.

Kicking a Ball

Try kicking a large rubber ball while on stilts. With a group of stilt-walkers, a game of soccer can be played. Cardboard boxes can be used for goals. A quick game of soccer is an ideal novelty for use in an act or demonstration.

Going Up and Down Stairs

Try walking up and down stairs on stilts. The stair platform, described under "Equipment" at the beginning of this chapter, can be used in an act. For example, walk up the stairs, pivot all the way around, then walk down. Stair hopping is another possibility. Going down is easiest. Hopping up stairs takes considerable practice, but it can be done.

BASIC ACTS

From the stilting skills described above, you can work up entertaining regular and clown acts.

Regular

This is intended only as a basic skeleton. The act can be done solo, or with two or more performers.

1. Walk out on stilts. Make rapid circles.
2. Walk sideways.
3. Walk backwards.
4. Pivoting on one stilt.
5. Hopping on first two, then one stilt.
6. Do stunts on stair platform, such as walking to top, pivoting around, and hopping down the stairs.
7. A finale, which can be done on taller stilts. This might be done on the stair platform. Regardless, the most spectacular feat should be used.

If the act has more than one performer, group stunts, such as Follow the Leader and a quick game of soccer, can be added. For dramatic effect, the act should build. Any special stunts that the performers can do should, of course, be worked into the act.

Clown

Stilts are ideal for clowning. The strap-on type is generally the most effective. Long pants can be made that will go over the stilts, and shoes can be added to the bottom of the stilts.

Clowning routines are covered in Chapter 20. Many of these can be adapted to stiltwalking.

chapter 7

BASIC TIGHTWIRE ARTISTRY

Tightrope walking, also called "funambulism," was done in ancient Egypt. During the Middle Ages it became a popular form of public entertainment. Tightrope walking acts have been an important part of circuses ever since their conception.

Jean Francois Gravelet, who used the pseudonym "Blondin," became famous for his tightrope walking across Niagara Falls in the 1850s. Many people believe that he was one of the greatest tightrope walkers ever.

Another famous performer is Karl Wallenda. In 1970 at the age of 65 he walked a wire suspended across the 750-foot-deep Tallulah Gorge in Georgia.

The term "tightwire" has largely replaced the earlier term "tightrope." Early walkers probably used a grass rope. Today wire ropes are generally used.

Our concern here will be with a wire suspended quite close to the ground. However, this still forms an exciting and challenging activity. After the basic skills have been mastered, an entertaining amateur act can be performed.

(Courtesy, Warren C. Wood)   *(Courtesy, Warren C. Wood)*

Deby Beemer practices on the tightwire at the Redlands YMCA to get ready for the Great Y Circus.   **Emily Melcher practicing on the tightwire at Redlands YMCA to prepare for the Great Y Circus.**

EQUIPMENT

An easy and inexpensive way to set up a tightwire is to suspend a wire cable between two trees. This assumes, however, that two suitable trees are available, which is not always the case. This rigging is more or less limited to one spot. To avoid injuring the trees, wooden backing blocks and/or a hose placed over the cable should be used where it goes around the trees.

Before going into other methods of rigging a tightwire, the wire itself needs to be considered. Although opinions vary, a half-inch diameter wire rope seems to be about right. This can be of plough steel or stainless steel and should be of a type with minimum stretch, such as 1 x 19 or 7 x 7 (these designate the number of smaller individual wires and their arrangement).

By purchasing thimbles and cable clamps along with the cable, you can do the rigging yourself, or you can have the wire made up for you at some hardware and most marine stores. When making your own cable attachments, it's a good idea to use two cable clamps in series for each connection, placing them a few inches apart. Suitable block and tackles and/or turnbuckles are readily available. If possible, have all cable cut to the correct lengths when you buy it, as this is difficult material to cut without the appropriate tool. Thimbles should be used where connections are made.

Several possible wire riggings are shown. Firm ground is needed for holding the stakes in the outdoor setup. In soft ground, the stakes can be set in concrete.

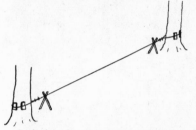

Basic tightwire set up between two trees.

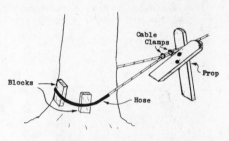

To avoid injuring trees, wooden backing blocks and/or hose are used. Prop is constructed of two pieces of 2 x 6 lumber bolted together.

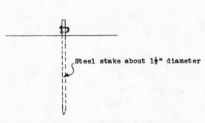

In firm ground a stake can be used for attaching tightwire rigging.

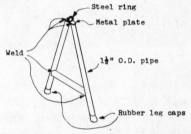

Basic construction of A-frame for tightwire rigging.

The wall attachment requires strong walls with large backing blocks. Before using this method, make certain that it will not damage the building.

For floor attachments, standard gymnastic plates or hooks can be used, but these should be chain-fastened to the concrete subfloor, not just screw-fastened to the wood floor. In some cases the plates for a horizontal bar can also be used for a tightwire.

The wire can be from about ten to twenty feet long. The recommended starting height is about one foot from the floor or ground. In some cases the height can be made adjustable. One, two, and three foot high capabilities are ideal. Unless the wire is over soft grass, mats or other soft landing surface should be used under the wire.

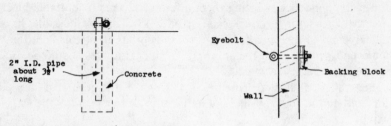

2" I.D. pipe about 3½' long

Concrete

Pipe with eyebolt for attachment of tightwire rigging. Pipe is set in ground in concrete.

Eyebolt

Backing block

Wall

Wall attachment for tightwire.

Floor attachment for tightwire.

Some professional wire acts use tightwires that do not require any wall or floor attachment. These independent units have a framework running under the wire, which presents a definite hazard for beginners. Thus, these riggings are recommended only for advanced tightwire walkers.

Standard gym and recreational clothing can be worn for wire walking, except special shoes are needed. Gymnastic shoes with non-slip soles can be used. Resin, available at sporting goods stores, is used on both the shoes and wire to help prevent slipping.

A bamboo pole about twelve feet long with a six pound weight firmly attached to each end will be of advantage as a balancing pole for the beginner. For the umbrella stunts a standard umbrella will work, but make sure it's an old one that can be sacrificed, as it is likely to be damaged during the learning process.

Also helpful are starting platforms at each end of the wire. For an act there should be a convenient place for special equipment, such as balancing poles and umbrellas. Stunts with a hoop are also given. A plastic hula hoop can be used for these.

Basic tightwire rigging.

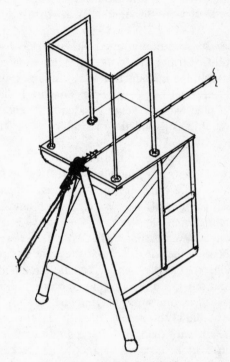

Starting platform for tightwire.

MECHANICS

In tightwire walking the base on which the body rests is reduced to a small width of wire in the side-to-side directions. The feet cannot be shifted sideways to another point to regain balance lost to the side, nor can the wire be shifted under the performer, assuming that the wire is rigid. There will be at least some play in the wire that is used by the more advanced performer to help maintain balance and perform stunts, but this will be ignored for the moment.

In order to understand how it is possible to maintain balance on such a narrow base, we will first consider the use of a balancing pole. When one is in balance on the wire while holding the pole, the pole is held horizontal as shown. If balance is lost to one side and the pole is kept horizontal to the ground, the body will continue to fall unless a correction is made. To regain balance, the pole is therefore rotated downward to the side that the body is falling. Since for every action there is an opposite and equal reaction, the body will thereupon rotate in the direction required to regain balance. By slightly over-compensating, the pole can then be brought back to its original horizontal position.

From this it can be seen that a long pole with heavy weights is advantageous, as this will give the pole a greater moment of inertia. Blondin, mentioned in the introduction to this chapter, used a 40-foot balancing pole for his tightrope feats across Niagara Falls.

If a lightweight pole without weights added to its ends is used, balance is much more difficult, but the mechanics of regaining balance are the same.

Without the balancing pole, the arms serve the same rotational functions. However, they are much less effective, making balance much more difficult. The arms are most effective when extended as far to the sides as possible. If heavy weights are held in the hands, maintaining balance becomes easier.

In this discussion it was assumed that both feet were on the wire with one ahead of the other and that the wire was perfectly taut. By standing on one foot, the other leg can be straddled to the side. This provides rotation, too, involving an opposite and equal action-reaction. Thus, this also comes into play in wire walking.

Slack in the wire allows the base to be shifted. However, walking a slack wire is more difficult than in walking a taut wire, so this actually adds to the difficulty of keeping balance. The mechanics involved become quite complex, so will not be considered further here.

Another aid to maintaining balance is an umbrella. The principle here is to trap air which, by movement of the umbrella in appropriate directions, serves to restore balance. Or, to state this more accurately, the air resists the movements of the umbrella, which provides a restoring force for maintaining balance, provided of course that it is properly applied.

Forward-backward balance is maintained in the same manner as walking.

Here are some tips for learning:

1. Begin with a low wire. About a foot high wire is ideal for learning the basic skills.

2. Tightwire walking is best learned in a step-by-step manner.

Learn each skill before going on to the next one.
  3. Concentrate on what you are doing.
  4. Never practice alone.
  5. Use resin on the wire and soles of shoes to avoid slipping.

BASIC SKILLS

With Balancing Pole

Begin with a balancing pole about twelve feet long with a six-pound weight firmly attached to each end.

Walking Forward

Start on platform, facing wire. Hold pole in center with hands about shoulder width apart and the back of the hands toward body. Notice that the pole can be rotated until it touches the ground. By resting the pole against the ground, retaining balance should be easy.

Step out onto the wire. If you start to lose balance to one side, rotate the pole in that direction until it rests against the ground. When balance is regained, bring the pole back to a horizontal position. Try to walk all the way across the wire.

By practicing in this manner, it should soon be possible to maintain balance without touching the pole to the ground. The rotations required for keeping balance are still the same.

In walking the feet should be placed almost straight ahead, with the wire between the big toe and the next one. The balancing pole should be carried about waist high. The body should be upright in good posture, but not stiff. Focus the eyes on the wire ahead. Do not look down at feet; the feet are positioned by feel.

Practice walking forward across the wire until it can be done repeatedly with control and without touching the balancing pole to the ground. Try to work in a smooth and relaxed manner. Avoid jerky movements.

When the opposite platform is reached, raise the pole overhead and turn body around so that starting position is again assumed. Then walk across the wire in the opposite direction.

Standing

Walk to center of wire, then try to maintain balance with both feet on the wire, one ahead of the other. The same rotations of the balancing

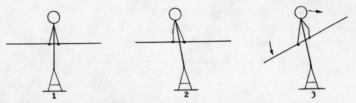

Basic mechanics of maintaining balance with balancing pole. 1) In balance, pole is horizontal to body. 2) If pole is kept horizontal to ground when balance is lost, body will continue to fall. 3) Balance is regained by rotating pole in direction of falling.

pole are required for corrections. Try to see how long balance can be maintained without moving feet. Finish the sequence by walking forward again.

Next try standing on one foot, with the other one to the side. Begin by walking to the center of the wire. Try to hold balance on one foot for as long as possible. This skill should also be learned on the other foot.

Walking Backwards

Begin by walking forward to past the center of the wire. Come to position standing on both feet. Take forward foot off wire and place it on wire again behind the other foot. Then take another half step backwards. Pause, then walk forward again.

Continue adding additional backward steps before returning to forward walking. Soon it should be possible to walk the length of the wire backwards. For this, start on one platform facing away from the wire with the pole held in front of the body. Walk backwards across wire to other platform.

Combinations of forward and backward walking and one and two foot standing can now be performed.

Turning Around

Walk to center of wire. With both feet on the wire, one ahead of the other, in a standing position, make a half turn by pivoting on the feet. For this stunt, it's important that there be room for the balancing pole to swing above the platforms and any stands or other parts of the rigging if the wire is so short that the pole extends over its ends. While the pivot is made, the pole is also turned around.

Stepping Over Balance Pole

You may want to skip this one for now and come back to it later. When you're ready to try it, walk to the center of the wire. Bend for-

| 1 | 2 | 3 |

Basic mechanics of maintaining balance with umbrella. 1) In balance, umbrella is held level. 2) If umbrella is held in same position when balance is lost, body will continue to fall. 3) Balance is regained by moving umbrella to side opposite direction of falling and pulling against air resistance.

ward with the pole, then step first one leg, then the other, over the pole until the pole is behind the back. Try to maintain standing balance in this position. Then step backwards over the pole, first with one foot, then the other one.

With Umbrella

The same basic progression is used, except instead of rotating the pole to keep balance, hold the umbrella in front with the handle at about face level. If balance is lost to the right side, move the umbrella to the left and pull quickly against the air resistance. If balance is lost to the left side, the correction is the opposite.

First learn to walk across the wire forward. Then try one and two foot stationary balancing. Next comes walking backwards. Finally, try turning around. This should be less awkward than with the long pole.

With Weights in Hands

Next try the same progression with a five pound weight in each hand. A pair of dumbbells can be used. Balance is maintained by rotation, as was done with the balance pole, only now it will be more difficult.

Without Balancing Aids

This time go through the same progression of stunts without any balancing aids. This will be much more difficult, so it may take a while to learn all of the stunts. But master each one before going on to the next one.

With Hoop

Here's a challenging stunt that's done with a hoop. With the hoop in one hand, walk to the center of the wire. Step through the hoop, one foot after the other, until both feet are inside the hoop. Circle the hoop, raising it on over the head. This can also be done the opposite direction. Circle the hoop on over the body from head down to feet, then step out of the hoop. Many variations are possible.

BASIC ACT

Our concern here is with an individual act. If more than one person, the same basic act can be used, except the parts should be divided up.

1. Do sequence with balancing pole. Start with easy stunts and build to those more difficult. Keep the act moving. Show each stunt, then go on. Always keep the audience wanting more.

2. Do sequence with umbrella.

3. Do sequence without balancing aids. A good finish from a wire up to about three feet from the ground is to face sideways and do a straddle jump dismount. A mat should be placed for landing. The techniques for doing a straddle jump are given in Chapter 15.

Since originality is important, other specific stunts have not been included. However, for those who would like a set act, here's one possibility.

1. With balancing pole, walk across forward to within a few feet of opposite platform, stop, walk backwards to near starting platform, walk forward to center of wire, hold stationary balance on two feet. Hold stationary balance on one foot, walk forward a couple of steps, step feet over pole, then back again. Walk forward to platform.

2. With umbrella, walk quickly across to opposite platform. Turn around on platform. Walk across forward to within a few feet of other end, walk backwards to center, hold standing balance on both feet and then on one foot. Walk forward a couple of steps, do pivoting half turn and walk quickly forward to platform.

3. Without any balancing aids, walk quickly across wire. Turn around and walk across to near other end. Do pivoting half turn, take a couple of steps forward, then do another pivoting turn. Walk forward to near platform, walk backwards to near other platform. Hold stationary balance on one foot. Walk quickly forward to platform.

4. With hoop, walk to center of wire. Hold stationary balance, then step through hoop and circle it upward overhead. Repeat circling hoop in opposite direction. Walk quickly forward to platform.

5. Without any balancing aids, walk to center of wire, turn sideways, and do straddle jump dismount.

(Courtesy, Steve McPeak)

Walking up the inclined wire. Steve McPeak is not from a circus family and he did not start learning circus skills until he was 20 years old.

If you have to jump down from the wire during a performance, go quickly back to a starting platform and continue at the point where you were. However, if all of the basic skills have been learned well, a miss should be rare.

chapter 8

UNICYCLE SKILLS

Historically, unicycling is a rather recent innovation. The idea that it was possible to ride balanced above one wheel probably came from riding penny-farthings, which were not freewheeling. Often the riders found themselves balanced on one wheel with the tiny rear wheel completely off the ground. This resulted from braking too rapidly. The wheel, controlled directly by the pedal action, would stop, but the rider would continue forward at a faster rate, often spilling off forward, but sometimes riding on one wheel for a time before the spill or, if he were lucky, having the rear wheel return to the ground.

Who was the first person to unicycle remains controversial, but in the 1870s and 1880s a number of cyclists, including Ahrens, Lou Lacher, Minting, George N. Hendee, Sebastian Merrill Neuhausen, William Dinwindle, and Howard Seely, all made claims of having been the first.

By the 1890s unicycling was a popular form of circus and stage entertainment. Many unusual feats were performed, and someone was always coming along who would top what had been done previously.

Here are some of the present unicycle records:

The longest recorded journey on a unicycle was made by Wally Watts of Edmonton, Canada, in 1973. He rode from Vancouver to Halifax, a distance of 4,550 miles, in three months and one day.

The tallest unicycle ever ridden to date measures 31 feet 2 inches from the bottom of the wheel to the top of the saddle. The feat was accomplished by Steve McPeak of Olympia, Washington, on February 2, 1969, in the parking lot behind Circus Circus Casino in Las Vegas.

In recent years unicycling has become a popular recreational activity and has found wide acceptance in amateur circuses. Manufactured unicycles are now readily available. With an average amount of physical ability and a sincere desire, it's generally possible to learn to ride a unicycle in a short period of time. Fundamental skills up to the point where a basic amateur act can be performed are included here. For a complete coverage of unicycling, including intermediate and advanced skills, the reader is referred to this author's *The Unicycle Book* (Stackpole Books, Cameron & Kelker Streets, Harrisburg, Pa. 17105). Another source of information is the Unicycling Society of America, Inc., 30246 S. Stockton Dr., Farmington, Michigan 48024. Membership is open to all interested unicyclists, and the membership fee of $3.00 per year covers membership card, subscription to the quarterly newsletter, and the right to vote in the annual election of officers.

EQUIPMENT

A heavy-duty unicycle is recommended. Many bicycle shops and chain stores now carry these. A unicycle with a 20-inch wheel and five or five and one-half inch pedal arms is generally best for learning. It is important, however, that the saddle height can be adjusted so that the rider's leg will be nearly extended to reach the pedal in the down position when he is mounted. The saddle should be curved unicycle type rather than a bicycle saddle, and the bearings should be sturdy and without play (wobble) between the axle and bearings. Unicycles built on the order of a tricycle are generally unsatisfactory. At the time of this writing good quality imported unicycles are available on the West Coast for about $25, and on the East Coast for about $35.

MECHANICS

Unicycling is possible because the rider has direct control for turning the wheel. Balance is maintained almost entirely by moving the unicycle wheel. There are two basic types of balance involved: side-to-side and forward-backward. When riding a unicycle, side-to-side balance is, for the most part, taken care of automatically, as is the case when riding an ordinary bicycle. Rotating wheels tend to remain balanced.

The main difficulty for the beginner is in learning the forward-backward balance, which is controlled almost entirely by the speed and direction of the pedaling. When riding forward, faster pedaling is used to counter too much forward lean and slower pedaling (braking) or pedaling backwards to counter too much backward lean. Or looking at it another way, if the center of gravity of the unicycle and rider is forward to the hub, faster pedaling is required to bring the wheel back under the rider. In turn, if the center of gravity falls behind the hub, slower pedaling or pedaling backwards is required to bring the center of gravity back over the hub.

By the time forward-backward balance is learned, side-to-side balance is generally automatic.

Turning is accomplished by action-reaction twisting. To turn to one side when riding forward, the arms and upper body are rotated the opposite direction (see Basic Turns). This is the basis for all turning initiated by the rider alone. A true spin is started by an outside force, such as by pushing against a wall or partner.

From the above discussion it can be seen that unicycling is a continual checking of incipient falling. With practice the correct patterns will become automatic and the rider will no longer have to think about them consciously.

A couple of other points should be mentioned. Good riding posture, which means the upper body in line with the unicycle frame and the head and shoulders up, will make riding much easier and should be practiced right from the start. Changing the shape of the upper body and flapping the arms will only make balance more difficult.

Other factors, such as fear, strength, coordination, and desire, are also important and will largely determine how long it will take to master the correct mechanics. While many people have learned to ride unicycles on their own, the step-by-step method given below can make learning much easier.

BASIC SKILLS

Adjust the saddle height so that, when mounted, the leg on the pedal in the lowest position will be nearly extended to reach the pedal. Make sure all bolts, especially the saddle clamps, are securely fastened.

For learning, a hard smooth surface adjacent to a curb is ideal. A 4- x 4-inch block of wood a couple of feet long can be used if no suitable curb is available. The curb or block is used to keep the unicycle wheel from rolling in one direction.

A slight incline can be used to advantage by a beginner, especially those who encounter difficulties in the initial steps. The incline will help to eliminate the dead spots in the pedaling cycles. Many beginners also find it helpful to let part of the air out of the tire. This will reduce the ease with which the cycle can twist and enable the rider to more fully concentrate on the important forward-backward balance.

Learning to Ride

Begin with two helpers. It isn't necessary that they know how to ride a unicycle. A curb or stop-block is also needed. With the unicycle and pedals positioned as shown, the wheel will be forced into the stop-block when pressure is applied to the down and back positioned pedal. Notice that the pedals can also be reversed. The position that feels best to the rider should be used, so try both ways to see which seems most natural.

The two helpers should stand directly to the rider's sides. The help is provided by holding hands rather than with locked arms or clasped wrists.

With the starting position assumed, the rider is ready to mount the unicycle. By keeping the weight on the pedal that is toward the stop-block, the wheel is forced against the block and will not roll out from under the rider. Step the foot from the ground to the forward pedal. Immediately assume an erect posture with the upper body in line with the unicycle frame and the head and shoulders up.

Retain this posture and pedal away from the stop-block. The two helpers walk along with the rider. Their main purpose is to provide side-to-side support to keep the rider from twisting. In this way the rider can concentrate on the forward-backward balance. The pattern to learn is: (1) speed the pedal action when losing balance forward, (2) slow the pedal action when losing balance backwards. It is important to retain an erect posture. Do not try to keep balance by rapid body motions, as this will only make learning more difficult.

With the two helpers used in this manner, it should be possible to ride without falling. To dismount, come to a stop with one pedal in a down position. Dismounting can be done either forward or backwards. The beginner can learn both methods, or backwards only, which seems to work best, especially in a limited space. To dismount forward, release the hand hold from one of the helpers and reach back and grip the back of the saddle. Step the foot on the upper pedal forward to the ground. In this way the rider lands on his feet and catches the unicycle. Catching the unicycle should become habit, as dropping it will cause damage. For dismounting backwards, release the hand hold from one of the helpers and reach forward and grip the front of the saddle. Step the foot on the upper pedal down and backwards to the ground. Remember, the dismount should be done from a complete stop with a pedal in the down position. Correct dismounting is controlled. It should be intentional, rather than a recovery from a fall.

Mounting and learning to ride with stop-block and two helpers.

Continue practicing with two helpers, each time starting with the aid of a stop-block (if needed), until control and confidence are gained. The rider should try to use only light finger pressure against the helpers' hands.

The next step is the same, except with one helper. Again, the helper should stand directly to the rider's side. Mount with the aid of the wheel-stop, then ride forward. Dismount as was done previously. Use the helper as little as possible.

At this point an experienced unicycle rider can ride along holding hands with the beginner, instead of having a walking helper. Also, it's possible for two beginners, neither of whom can ride alone, to ride together holding hands.

After a day or two with one helper, most riders are ready to solo. Begin by using one helper to mount. This should now be possible in the open without the curb or stop-block. Then ride forward alone. Dismounting should be done as previously. Remember to catch the unicycle.

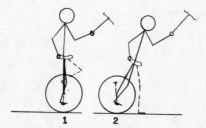

Dismounting forward. 1) Grasp back of saddle with one hand.2) Step off forward. Holding hand of one helper is shown. Dismounting alone is basically the same.

This skill should be practiced until at least fifty feet, and preferably a block, can be covered with control. Then it's time to go on to stunt riding.

Dismounting backwards. 1) Grasp front of saddle with one hand. 2) Step off backwards. Holding hand of one helper is shown. Dismounting alone is basically the same.

Mounting with Stop-block

Mount the unicycle as was done previously with the aid of the stop-block or curb, only this time without the helper. After mounting, ride forward for at least 50 feet before dismounting.

Mounting in open.

Riding Between Lines

Mount and ride forward, only this time between lines two feet apart. The lines can be made with chalk on pavement or concrete. Masking tape can be used on gym floor.

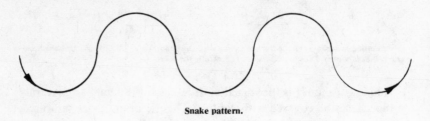

Snake pattern.

Basic Turns

Mount and ride forward as was done previously. Make a quarter turn, first one direction and then, after riding straight forward again, the other direction. Turns are made by turning the arms and upper body in the direction opposite to the desired turn. Most riders at this stage, however, can make turns without thinking about or even being aware of the mechanics.

Complete Circle

Ride in a complete circle approximately 20 feet in diameter. Learn to do this in both directions. Gradually work down to smaller circles.

Mounting in Open

Position the unicycle as was done with the stop-block. On the initial attempts use a helper. This time the wheel will roll backwards, so the foot must be brought quickly from the ground to the forward pedal. Ride forward.

Practice until you can mount the unicycle in the open without help.

Figure Eight Pattern

At this point patterns such as the Figure Eight should not present any special difficulties. Other possibilities are snake patterns and loops in alternate directions.

Figure Eight pattern.

Rocking

Rocking is a half-pedal action, alternately forward and backwards. It can be done two ways, that is, with either pedal forming the half-circle in the down position.

To learn, ride forward, pause, half-pedal backwards, then ride forward again. Practice this until it can be done both ways, i.e., starting with either pedal forward.

Next try the same thing, only with two rocking motions in succes-

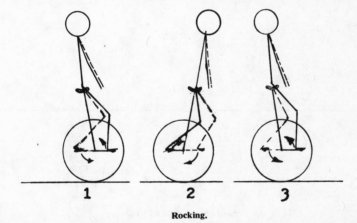

Rocking.

sion. Continue practice by adding additional rocking motions until ten or more can be done in a row. Repeat with the feet in the opposite position.

Riding Backwards

Ride backwards with one helper, holding one hand only. The helper should be directly to the rider's side. Begin by riding forward, pausing, then pedaling backwards. Ride backwards for at least 25 feet with no pauses or rocking.

Next try riding backwards for 25 feet alone. Pause or ride forward before dismounting. Continue practice until riding backwards can be done smoothly.

Backward Turns

Ride backwards and make quarter turns in each direction.

Backward Circles

Make circles approximately twenty feet in diameter while riding backwards. Learn to circle both directions. Gradually work down to smaller circles.

Backward Figure Eight

Ride backwards and perform a Figure Eight pattern. Try to go through the pattern more than one time.

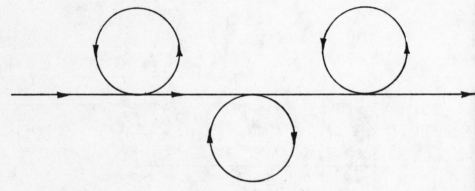

Loops in alternate directions.

PARTNER STUNTS

Partner stunts add to the fun of unicycling. Included here are the basic patterns. From these, hundreds of combinations are possible.

Holding Hands Facing Same Direction

Two riders unicycling forward in same direction join hands, then ride along together holding hands. Try coming to a complete stop and hold balance for one minute without rocking. Ride forward again.

Next try mounting while holding hands. Ride forward. More difficult is to mount and, without rocking more than once, hold stationary balance for one minute.

Other variations are the rocking pattern while holding hands and circle and Figure Eight patterns. Also try riding backwards. To do this, ride forward while holding hands, pause, then ride backwards.

Holding Hands Facing Opposite Directions

Two riders approach from opposite directions. Grasp hands and begin circling. Riders should lean away from each other. Notice that each rider goes forward in same direction around circle. Release hands and continue riding separately.

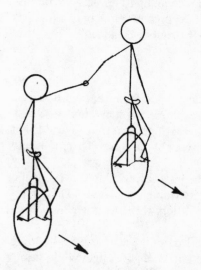
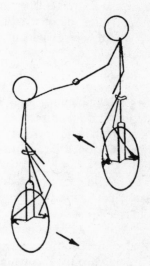

Holding hands facing same direction.   **Holding hands facing opposite directions.**

Combinations

From the two basic hand-holding positions, a number of combinations can be performed. Here are some that you will want to try.

Ride forward holding hands, with both riders facing the same direction. On signal, one rider spins the other one-half turn, releasing hand hold and grasping hands again facing opposite directions. Do four or five circle patterns, then repeat half-spin of one rider and rejoin hand-holding facing the same direction and with both riders pedaling forward.

Another combination is for both partners to ride holding hands facing the same direction. On signal, one rider spins partner one half-turn. The rider who did the turn then rides backwards while the other rider continues forward. A second half-spin returns both riders to forward riding.

More difficult are full under-arm turns. Begin with both riders facing the same direction. One rider does a full turn under other rider's arm while retaining hand contact, similar to turns done in square dancing.

BASIC ACTS

With the above skills, entertaining solo and partner acts can be performed. Hundreds of combinations are possible, but only skeletons are included here. Originality should, of course, be added.

One Person

Begin by mounting unicycle on stage. Ride forward, then do circle patterns, first one direction, then the other. Do each stunt just long enough to show it, then go on to the next one. Next do Figure Eight pattern. Continue through pattern two or three times. Dismount and pause.

Mount, ride forward, and then begin rocking. After rocking ten times, ride forward again. Switch to riding backwards. Do circles while riding backwards, first one direction, then the other. Ride forward again and dismount. Pause.

End with most difficult feat. To this point the act has been building in difficulty, so the finale must stand out. A Figure Eight while riding backwards, for example, would work well. Show the trick, then finish quickly.

This completes the basic act. Within this framework, special stunts can easily be added. Give the act dramatic effect by keeping it moving and not repeating stunts too many times. Show each trick, then go on. The pauses are for applause and resting.

With Partner

Follow the same basic format, except work in partner stunts between solos. Since there are times when only one person is per-

(Courtesy, Jim Smith)

Riding a unicycle over a teeter board. A performer in the Hamilton Mini Circus.

forming, rest is possible without slowing the act. Doing some of the individual stunts in Follow the Leader fashion is another possibility. It's important that the act be worked out carefully and that each performer knows exactly what he is to do. The act should keep moving with the only pauses being for applause. Making each sequence more difficult than the one before generally gives the best dramatic effect.

chapter 9

CIRCUS BICYCLING

With the invention of the "safety" bicycle, a number of professional cycle acts were formed. Early bicycles of the chain-driven type were direct drive (i.e., they were not freewheeling). This made them ideal for trick riding, as they could be ridden on one wheel like a unicycle and backwards.

Famous early acts were performed by Sebastian Merrill Neuhausen, who performed all over the world in the 1890s, and N. R. Kaufmann of Rochester, New York, who was one of the first Americans to perform in Europe. Bicycle acts continue to be popular in the circuses of today.

World championships are held in artistic bicycling in Europe. The sport is especially popular in Czechoslovakia, Germany, and Switzerland. The bicycles used are similar to the special bicycles described in this chapter.

Bicycling makes an ideal amateur act. Those watching generally don't realize that a special bicycle is being used and often will go home and try the stunts they have seen on a regular bicycle, only to find that they can't do them.

(Courtesy, William Jenack)
Circus bicycle used by professional performer
Willie Richie. Bicycle is now owned by
William Jenack, who supplied photo and
dimensions.

A standard bicycle that has been converted to
circus bicycle.

EQUIPMENT

Several types of stock bicycles can be converted to circus bicycles, or you can have them special built. Two firms that will do this are Hamilton's Bicycle Store, 1622 South Parkwood Lane, Wichita, Kansas 67218; and City Cyclery, 670 Mentor Ave., Painesville, Ohio 44077.

To make your own, a sturdy bicycle with narrow tires is recommended. The bicycle size should be the same as would ordinarily be ridden. Smaller wheel sizes, such as 24-inch wheels, are often used by professional performers. Dimensions of one circus bicycle used by a professional performer are given.

The modifications required to convert a regular bicycle are to remove all attachments such as fenders, lights, kickstands, and chain guards from the bicycle, straighten the front fork, modify the saddle, and convert the drive to a direct drive with a one-to-one gear ratio.

It also helps to use shorter crank arms, those from five to six inches in length being preferred. This can easily be done on the type of bicycle with the crank arms connected to the axle with crank-arm pins. Simply remove the long crank arms and add shorter ones.

The drive conversion involves replacing the large front sprocket with one to match that on the rear wheel. A solid mounted sprocket is needed on the rear wheel. This can be done by replacing the present hub with one that has a solid mounted sprocket (available through bicycle shops) or by welding the present sprocket to the hub. If the hub has a brake system, remove brake components so that the hub will spin freely on the axle.

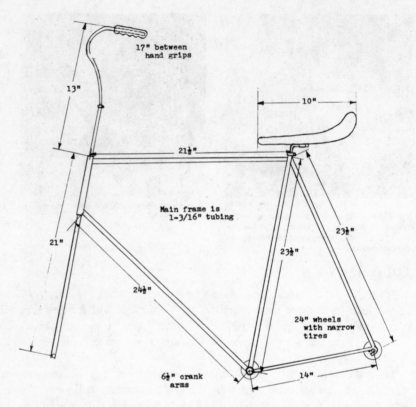

17" between
hand grips

13"

10"

21½"

Main frame is
1-3/16" tubing

23½"

21"

23½"

24½"

24" wheels
with narrow
tires

6½" crank
arms

14"

Dimensions of Willie Richie's circus bicycle.

Next, replace the large front sprocket with one that matches the back sprocket. To do this, remove the crank-arm pin on the sprocket side and remove the crank arm. The large sprocket can be removed by grinding off the upset portion on the inside of the crank arm and then driving sprocket off the splined boss of the crank arm. The small sprocket is then centered in position. This is important. If the sprocket is not centered and lined up exactly, the bicycle will be difficult to use, as there will be slack in the chain during part of each pedal cycle. The sprocket is welded in place, and the pedal arm is installed back on the axle.

The chain will have to be shortened. Remove connecting link, saw extra links from chain, and replace connecting link. Reassemble bicycle chain and wheel assembly.

To straighten the front fork, remove it from the bicycle. The fork can then be straightened by heating it with a torch or without heating by fastening it in a vice between blocks of wood, as shown, and slowly

Method for straightening bicycle fork without heating.

straightening it with a section of pipe over the ends of the fork prongs. Replace the fork to the bike.

The saddle needs to have additional curve and be placed farther back than on a regular bicycle. An L-shaped saddle post angled toward the back of the bicycle can be used for mounting the saddle. A regular bicycle saddle can be modified as shown for use on a circus bicycle.

This completes the assembly except for any necessary painting. For use in an act, the bicycle frame might be painted silver or chrome-plated at a shop.

MECHANICS

The mechanics of riding a circus bicycle are similar to a regular bicycle, except that many additional tricks can be done. The direct drive allows direct control of the rear wheel. The bicycle can be pedaled backwards. It can also be ridden on one wheel like a unicycle. For this the mechanics are the same as for the unicycle (see Chapter

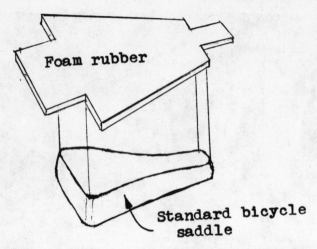

A regular bicycle saddle can be modified for use on a circus bicycle by taping a layer of ½"
foam rubber in place.

8). For learning to ride a circus bicycle on one wheel, it's a good idea to learn to ride a unicycle first.

The best method for learning tricks on a circus bicycle is generally in a step-by-step manner, beginning with the easiest skills. Learn each one before going on to the next one.

Always wear shoes when practicing on a circus bicycle. Shoes with heels to help keep the feet on the pedals will make things easier during the beginning stages.

BASIC SKILLS

Adjust the saddle height so that, when mounted, the leg on the pedal in the lowest position will be nearly extended to reach the pedal. Make sure that all bolts on the bicycle are firmly fastened down.

The best·place to practice is on a hard smooth surface with plenty of open space. This can be concrete, asphalt, or a wooden gym floor.

Riding Forward and Turning

Mount and ride forward. This is the same as on a regular bicycle, except that the gear ratio is one-to-one. Braking is by slowing the pedal action. This may feel strange at first.

Next try turns while riding forward. First try large circle turns, then work down to smaller ones. Try continuous circles, making the circles as small as possible. Other possibilities are Figure Eights and serpentine patterns.

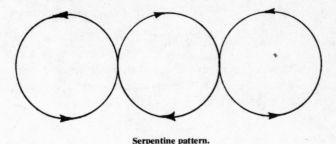

Serpentine pattern.

Balancing in One Place

Ride forward and come to standstill. Maintain balance by moving pedals backwards and forward as little as possible. Control of the front wheel can also be used to help maintain balance. Turn the wheel towards the direction the bicycle is falling.

Spinning Front Wheel

Begin as above. While maintaining balance in one place, spin the handlebars. Begin with a half-turn of the front wheel. Then try a full turn. Follow a handlebar grip around with one hand.

Riding Backwards

This may require considerable practice. Begin by riding forward and coming to a standstill. Then make one full pedal backwards. Come to standstill and pedal forward again. Keep adding an addition full pedal backwards on each attempt.

The steering is now similar to rudder control of a sailboat. It may take a while to get used to this. Continue practicing until fifty feet can be ridden backwards with control. Use a slow even speed.

Turns with Backward Riding

After learning to ride backwards in a straight line, start adding gradual turns. Work up to sharper ones. Learn to turn both directions.

Circles with Backward Riding

Try a large circle first. Gradually work down to smaller ones. It may take a while to learn this. Then start over again with a large circle to the opposite direction and work down to smaller ones.

Figure Eight with Backward Riding

Begin with a large Figure Eight pattern. When this can be performed with control, try a smaller Figure Eight. Notice that turns must be made in both directions to do this skill.

Riding on One Wheel

Although it isn't absolutely necessary, it helps to be able to ride a unicycle. Begin by riding slowly forward. Press down hard on one

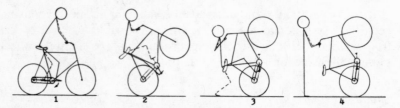

Begin by riding slowly forward. 1) Press down hard on one pedal while leaning backwards and pulling on the handlebars. 2) Ride the bicycle over the back wheel. 3 and 4) Dismount backwards to a stand on the ground, holding bicycle by handlebars.

pedal while leaning backwards and pulling on the handlebars. Ride the bicycle over the back wheel and dismount backwards to a stand on the ground, holding the bicycle by the handlebars.

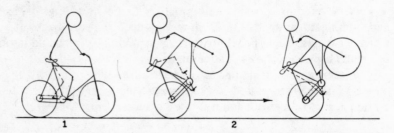

Riding circus bicycle on one wheel.

Practice this a number of times. When it can be done with control, try the same action, only easier. Once the front wheel is in the air, try to continue riding forward on the back wheel. If balance is lost backwards, dismount as was done previously. If balance is lost forward, try to continue pedaling so that the front wheel will land softly.

Continue practicing in this manner until long distances can be covered on one wheel. After fifty feet can be ridden with control, turns can be attempted.

Turns while Riding on One Wheel

The mechanics are the same as turning on a unicycle (see Chapter 8). First try gradual turns, one direction and then the other. Work up to quarter and then half-turns. Try zigzag patterns.

Circles while Riding on One Wheel

Try a large circle first. Then work down to smaller ones. Then repeat with circles in the opposite direction.

Figure Eight on One Wheel

Try a large Figure Eight first. Then work down to a smaller pattern.

Spinning Handlebars on One Wheel

While riding on one wheel, spin the handlebars. To do this follow one hand around with the handlebar grip. Or give the handlebars a spin and let them go free.

Rocking on One Wheel

Ride forward on one wheel. Come to standstill. Pedal one-half turn of the wheel backwards. Pedal forward again. This is one rocking motion. When this can be done, add a second rock. Continue practicing in this manner until a number of rocks can be made.

Repeat the learning procedure with the other pedal forward.

Riding Backwards on One Wheel

Ride forward on one wheel and come to a standstill. Ride backwards one complete pedal cycle. Ride forward again. Gradually add additional backward pedal cycles. After fifty feet can be covered riding backwards on one wheel in a straight line, try turns. Riding backwards on one wheel is a fairly advanced skill, so don't be discouraged if you don't learn it right away. You may also want to try complete circles and Figure Eights while riding backwards on one wheel.

Other Stunts

The basic stunts have been given above. There are a number of others. These include sitting backwards on the handlebars with feet on pedals and riding; riding while pedaling with one foot; and pedaling with one hand while sitting on the lower frame bar. In addition, you will probably have many original ideas of your own.

BASIC ACT

In many situations there will be only a small space. It's generally best to work up an act that can be done in a small area. In shows where there's more space, such as on a gym floor, stunts that can't be done in a small area can be added.

Begin act by riding forward and doing circle and Figure Eight patterns. Hold balance in one place. Spin front wheel. Ride forward again. Stop. Dismount. Pause.

Mount. Ride forward. Change to backward riding. Do circle and Figure Eight patterns. Change to forward riding. Stop. Dismount. Pause.

Mount. Ride forward. Change to forward riding on one wheel. Do circle and Figure Eight patterns. Change to forward riding on two wheels. Stop. Dismount. Pause.

Mount. Ride forward. Change to forward riding on one wheel. Spin handlebars. Rocking on one wheel. Ride forward on one wheel. Change to riding backwards on one wheel. If circles can be made, do these. If not, ride backwards to limits of working area, then change to forward riding. Change to riding on two wheels and dismount.

chapter 10

TUMBLING

Historically, tumbling is very old. In Egypt pictures were made depiciting tumbling stunts in the period 2100-2000 B.C., and it is likely that tumbling dates back to long before this. Tumbling is one of the most spectacular of all the circus skills and is also basic to the performance of many other acts.

A number of tumblers, both amateur and professional, have done double backward somersaults in ground tumbling, starting from build-up sequences, such as a round-off, flip-flap (backward handspring). Perhaps the greatest feat ever accomplished from feet-to-feet was a backward full fliffus (a double backward somersault with a full twist). It was done by Hal Holmes, an amateur tumbling champion at the University of Illinois. He did it first on April 22, 1963, using a round-off, flip-flap as a build-up sequence. To date, no one else has done this stunt.

Tumbling differs from balancing and pyramids (covered in separate chapters) in that tumbling is movement, that is, the creation and control of momentum. It's never stationary or in balance, such as a handstand. Tumbling is a fun activity, and there are stunts that can be done alone, and others that can be performed with one or more partners.

EQUIPMENT

Tumbling can be done on soft grass, but it's much safer to learn on tumbling mats. Most schools, YMCAs, and recreation centers have these. All of the basic stunts and acts detailed in this chapter can be done on a twenty-foot long mat, but one twenty-five or thirty feet long would be better. The mat should be at least five feet wide and from two to five inches thick.

Regular gym or recreational clothing are worn for tumbling, except that tennis or basketball shoes aren't suitable. You can go barefooted or, better yet, purchase a pair of soft-soled tumbling shoes. The kind with rubber soles are best, as the ones with leather soles tend to slip.

For more advanced tumbling, various items of spotting equipment are frequently used. However, for the basic skills shown here, you won't need any special equipment.

MECHANICS

At first, all tumbling stunts may look more or less the same. But soon it will be noticed that there are different types of stunts, such as rolls and handsprings, and that tumbling can be done forward, backwards, and sideways. There are also twisting stunts, and ones that start one direction and end another.

Since there are many different mechanical principles involved, they will be covered as needed with the individual stunts.

Safety is a most important consideration. Here are some basic rules:

1. Never practice alone.
2. Concentrate on what you are doing.
3. Start with the easiest skills first. Learn each one before going on to the next one.
4. Always warm-up before doing actual tumbling stunts. The warm-up should be for at least fifteen minutes. A suggested sequence is included in Chapter 3. Remember, circus tumblers warmup before doing their act. This is the part that you don't normally see. It's done backstage.

A few misconceptions need to be cleared up at this point. Tumbling requires a reasonably high level of physical fitness if it is to be safely performed. Fitness is derived from tumbling, but it's important to be reasonably fit *before* starting tumbling. Those who are extremely overweight or weak in proportion to their body weight should *not* attempt tumbling stunts. For these people it just isn't worth the risk. Besides, there are other circus skills such as juggling and unicycling that are much more suitable.

After learning the basic tumbling stunts shown in this chapter, many will want to go on to more difficult ones. For this, an experienced tumbling coach is highly recommended.

BASIC SKILLS

Individual Stunts

Some beginners will be able to learn these stunts quickly, others more slowly. The stunts are arranged in the order that they should be learned. Master each one before going on to the next one. Remember, warm up at least fifteen minutes before starting the actual tumbling practice.

Forward Roll

Assume the squat stance with the knees together and the hands placed as shown. The hands should be shoulder distance apart with the fingers pointed straight forward. The head should be bent forward, with the chin on the chest.

Roll forward by straightening the legs to raise the hips overhead. The bend at the hips should be maintained. This is important. Push against the mat so that most of the weight is held by the hands. Move hands from the mat to the shins. This is a "tuck" position. Continue the roll until on feet in a position similar to starting stance, except hands are on shins.

If difficulty is encountered in rolling to feet, take a position on the back, holding the shins in a tuck position. Then begin rocking back and forth. Continue until enough momentum is gained to come to the feet while still holding the tuck position with the hands on the shins. Each time try to make it to the feet with less rocks. Then go back to the complete forward roll again.

It's important to start the roll from the squat stance. Rolls from a stand and diving rolls will be covered later.

Forward roll.

Series of forward rolls.

Backward roll.

Series of backward rolls.

Diving forward roll.

Series of Forward Rolls

After learning one forward roll, a series is easy. Start with a forward roll, ending on the feet with the hands on the shins, as was done previously. Reach forward and place the hands on the mat. Notice that the position is now the same as was used at the beginning of a single forward roll. From this position, do a second forward roll. Then repeat the same thing, doing a third roll.

Notice that a series is done by repeating the same actions over and over. Remember that each roll starts with the hands on the mat with the fingers forward and the knees together inside the arms. The hands hold the shins in a tuck position on each roll. Make sure that the hands are placed on the mat *before* starting the next roll. Try to do the series smoothly and with control. At this point it's all right to pause between each roll. Make sure the starting position, as shown, is assumed between each roll. Common difficulties are forgetting to put the hands down between rolls and not assuming the tuck position during the roll. Notice that the hands do not contact the mat during the roll up from the back to the squat stand.

Backward Roll

The starting position is the same as for the forward roll. Notice that the hands are placed the same way, with the fingers pointing straight forward. With the chin forward against the chest, give a slight push with the hands. The tuck position should be maintained. With the elbows held close together, the fingers are placed close to the shoulders. The hands should be flat on the mat. Roll on over backwards, pushing the hands against the mat and maintaining the tuck position. Do not try shooting your legs into the air, as this can result in falling. The knees should not touch the mat. The finishing position is the same as the start.

Common difficulties are not holding the tuck and incorrect hand placement. Notice that the fingers are pointed toward the shoulders and the hands are placed flat with the elbows held close together. The momentum for the roll should come from the slight push with the hands, not from a leg kick.

Series of Backward Rolls

After learning one backward roll, a series shouldn't be any more difficult. Begin by doing a backward roll. The ending should be the same as the starting position. Pause, then push slightly with the hands and do a second backward roll. Then a third one. With practice, the slight pauses between rolls can be eliminated. Control is more important, however, than speed at this stage of learning.

Diving Forward Roll

Several steps will be used to lead up to this. First, start from a stand. Quickly assume starting position for a forward roll—that is, a squat stance with the knees together and the hands placed flat on the mat with the fingers pointed forward. Pause. Then do a forward roll. On each attempt, shorten the pause until the roll can be done smoothly from the stand.

Next, walk forward. Bring one knee up and land on both feet in a standing position. The feet should be about a foot apart. Pause. Assume forward roll starting position. Then do forward roll. Practice this sequence until it can be done with only a slight pause.

This time go back to the original starting position in a squat stance, only hold arms extended in front instead of placing them on the mat. Reach the hands forward about a foot and place them flat on the mat with the fingers pointed forward. At the same time push with the legs to roll the hips over the head and finish with the tuck and roll to the feet, as was done previously. Each time add additional dive to the roll. When this can be done with confidence, you're ready to try it from a walk. On the first attempts, come to a complete stop on both feet, pause, and then do the roll by reaching out forward with the hands. As practice is continued the pause can gradually be eliminated.

Gradually, generally over a period of several weeks, work up to the point where a run can be used instead of a walk. Notice that the diving roll is done from a two-foot take-off, without a skip-step. Later on some stunts will be done from a one-foot take-off, with a skip-step.

As confidence is gained, a longer dive can be used. This involves reaching out forward farther, with a more vigorous extension of the legs.

Cartwheel

The cartwheel can be done to either side. Do it whichever way feels the most natural. Most right-handed tumblers prefer to do it as shown. In this way they can do twisting stunts from right to left (counter-clockwise) and the foot steps will come out right. If the cartwheel is done the opposite way, then twisting should be from left to right (clockwise).

Begin with a chalk line down the center of the mat. Stand as shown. Place the forward hand on the mat ahead of the forward foot. Place the other hand on the mat ahead of the first one. Step the back foot around to the side past both hands to the line. Step the other foot around, turning the body *outward*. The last foot lands past the one that was stepped around past the arms first. If everything was done correctly, the ending should be the same as the starting position. At this stage the stepping is around to the side and done slowly.

After practicing this a number of times, try standing sideways with

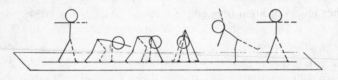

First step in learning cartwheel.

the arms out to the sides, as shown. Rock back and forth. Then reach forward and execute the cartwheel. On the first attempts, the legs can go around to the side. Gradually bring the legs more overhead until a cartwheel can be done with the legs extended and straddled directly above the head. This may require considerable practice.

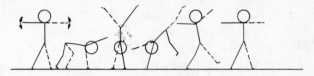

From standing sideways, rock back and forth and cartwheel.

Series of Cartwheels

Start standing sideways. Execute first cartwheel as was done previously. The ending should be the same as the start. Rock back and forth a couple of times and then do another cartwheel. With practice, the rocking will no longer be necessary. Gradually work up to the point where three or four cartwheels can be done without pausing between them. The hands and feet should be on a line down the center of the mat with a one-two-three-four rhythm.

Skip-step into Cartwheel

Stand sideways. With feet in same spots, twist them until the toes are pointed forward down the mat. Turn the shoulders and upper body forward and place both arms upward in front of the body. Do a cartwheel from this starting position. The ending should be sideways, as was done previously.

Take the same forward facing position again, only this time lift the forward foot a few inches off the mat. Skip forward on the back foot and place the forward foot down on the mat. Do cartwheel.

Next try the same sequence from a walk. Walk forward, skip-step as the other foot is brought forward and placed on the mat, and cartwheel. With practice, this can also be done from a short brisk run, that is, run, skip-step, and cartwheel.

Also try the run, skip-step sequence into a series of cartwheels. When done correctly, the performer travels down the mat in a straight line with a smooth even rhythm.

Skip-step into cartwheel.

Round-off

Begin facing forward with the front foot a few inches off the mat. Skip-step on the back foot and place the front foot down. Start a cartwheel action, only place the hands closer together. Bring the feet together in the air. Land on both feet in the direction opposite from the start.

Next try the round-off from a walk and skip-step. Work up to the point where it can be done from a short brisk run.

Skip-step into roundoff.

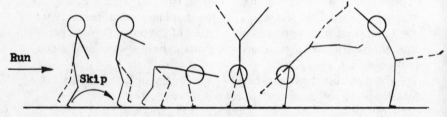

Skip-step into cartwheel step-out.

Round-off into Backward Roll

On the first attempts, pause after the round-off before doing the backward roll. The hands can be placed at the sides as the sit-back is made. Also try a round-off into a series of backward rolls.

Cartwheel Step-out

Begin with a skip step into a cartwheel. Turn out forward as the landing is made. Next try a cartwheel step-out into a round-off. Do this without a skip-step between the cartwheel and round-off. Also try a cartwheel, round-off, backward roll sequence.

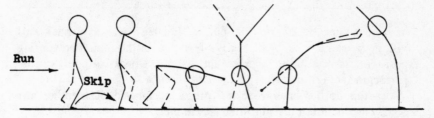

Skip-step into square-off.

Square-off

This is similar to the cartwheel step-out, except the landing is on both feet and facing straight forward. Also try a square-off into a forward roll. Another combination is a cartwheel step-out, square-off, forward roll series.

Partner Stunts

The partners should be about the same size and weight. They should both be able to do the individual stunts described above up to at least the cartwheel.

Forward Roll

Assume the starting position as shown. Performer A bends forward and places B's feet on the mat. A then does a forward roll, bringing B to a stand. This is the starting position, except the places have been reversed. Continue with a second roll.

With practice a smooth series can be done the length of the mat. Important points are maintaining holds on partners' ankles and, before rolling, placing partner's feet in close.

Backward Roll

Starting position is the same as for partner forward roll, except this time mat space is needed for going backwards. Performer A sits back

Two-person forward roll.

in a bent-knee backward roll, pulling **B**'s legs over in a backward roll at the same time. **A** places **B**'s feet flat on the mat. The starting position has now been reversed and a second backward roll can be performed.

Practice until a smooth series can be performed. Remember, the holds on partners' ankles must be maintained.

An effective combination is to do a series of partner forward rolls the length of the mat, then reverse directions and return with backward rolls.

Two-person backward roll.

Backward roll with partner assist.

Backward Roll with Partner Assist

For this stunt it's important that the tumbler doing the roll be able to do an individual backward roll with good arm support. Assume the starting position shown. **A** pushes down on **B**'s legs to signal that the pitch will follow. At first a low regular backward roll is done. With practice this can gradually be replaced with an extension roll, with flight between the hands and feet.

An interesting way to end the partner forward roll series is to release partner's legs as roll begins. A does a regular forward roll to feet. B remains on back. A comes to a stand, turns around, walks back to B, and grasps partner's ankles. Backward roll with partner assist is then executed.

Group Stunts

We will now consider stunts with three or more performers. These maneuvers will add variety to a tumbling act.

Three-person Side Roll Pattern

Assume the starting position shown. The center performer signals the start with, "Ready, begin." The center performer then does a log roll to the left, while person to his left leaps over him and then does a log roll. Person on opposite end leaps and does log roll, and so on. The things to remember are that on the ends a leap over comes first, followed by a log roll. Continue the pattern two or three times through. Have a preplanned stopping point so that everyone comes to a halt at the same time.

Leap and log roll sequence used in three and five person side roll patterns.

Starting sequence for three person side roll pattern.

Five-person Side Roll Pattern

Assume the starting position shown. One performer signals the start. Each person begins with the movement indicated by the arrows. After the start each performer alternates leaps and log rolls until he reaches the end. The end positions always leap inward. Continue the pattern through two or three times. Have a preplanned stopping point.

Starting sequence for five person side roll pattern.

Three-person Forward Roll Pattern.

This is the same as the three-person side roll pattern, except the leaps are straddle jumps and the log rolls forward rolls. The rolls should be low and short, with a tight tuck. This will make them easy for the straddle jumps. Each performer must know the routine, that is, after the start rolls are alternated with straddle jumps. The ends always jump inward.

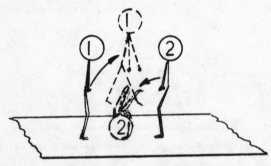

Straddle jump over, forward roll under. This is the basis for the three and five person forward roll patterns.

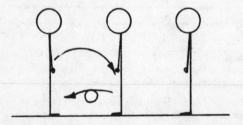

Starting sequence for three person forward roll pattern.

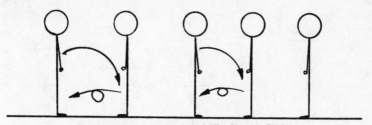

Starting sequence for five person forward roll pattern.

Five-person Forward Roll Pattern

Begin as shown. After the start the same rules as for the three-person forward roll pattern are followed.

Dive Roll Over Straddle Headstand

This requires one person who can do a headstand (the techniques for doing this are covered in Chapter 11). The straddle headstand is held as shown, with back to other performers. Other performers then each run and do dive roll over. When person ahead lands on two feet for take-off, next performer starts run.

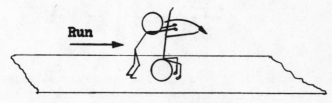

Dive roll over straddle headstand.

Dive Roll Over Crash Pyramid

Form a pyramid, as shown (the techniques for doing this are covered in Chapter 12). Tumbler who can do best dive roll runs toward pyramid. Just before take-off for dive roll (on signal from bottom man on side of pyramid of approach for dive roll), everyone in the pyramid straightens out, extending arms forward and legs backward. Everyone must do this at the same time for the best effect. The dive roll is done over the "crashed" pyramid.

Once the timing is worked out so that the pyramid crashes at the last instant, just when the dive roll is started, you will have a stunt that works well in shows.

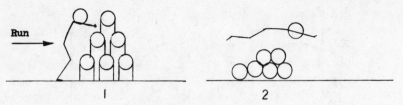

Dive roll over crash pyramid.

BASIC ACT

Since a good individual act is extremely difficult to perform, our concern here will be with a group act. For this at least seven tumblers will be needed, and the act works well with up to about a dozen performers.

1. Begin with crossing stunts, as shown. Half of the performers start on each end. If an uneven number, the extra person can be on either end. The extra person performs the same stunts, only alone. The stunts are done side-by-side in unison. One person acts as starter.

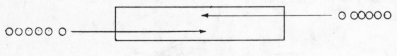

Basic crossing pattern.

When he goes, the person in the other line also starts. After the first person in each line, the others start when person ahead first contacts mat. After each stunt, line up on the opposite end of the mat. Do the following stunts: a) diving forward roll, b) cartwheel, c) round-off, d) cartwheel step-out, e) square-off, and f) round-off into backward roll. Each stunt is done with the appropriate run and take-off. It will take some experimenting to determine the starting point for each stunt for the best crossing effect. This part of the act should move rapidly.

2. Dive roll over six-person crash pyramid.

3. All performers line up at one end of the mat, except one, who does a straddle headstand. All others follow, one after the other, and dive roll over him.

4. Do the following double stunts: a) forward partner roll, b) backward partner roll, and c) backward roll with partner assist. Each sequence need be done only once. When two performers finish one stunt, the next two are ready to begin. This will keep the act moving.

5. Do five-person side roll pattern. Go all the way through three times. Stop, stand, and pause.

6. Same five persons do forward roll-straddle jump pattern.

7. All performers line up at one end of the mat. Each person does a series sequence the full length of the mat. Line up at the other end and do a second sequence down the mat. These should move rapidly and demonstrate a variety of stunts and combinations. If some performers can do stunts more difficult than those described in this chapter, such as headsprings and handsprings, these can be included too. However, use only those stunts that can be done well.

8. A good finish is a pyramid, such as the standing three-two-one, described in Chapter 12. Everyone in the act should be part of this, so work the ones not in the main pyramid into smaller pyramids and/or balance positions at the sides or in front. It's important that the pyramid be quickly formed. Hold for about six seconds. Then disassemble. Bow.

This basic act can be done in a number of styles, from formal to informal. The informal with lots of fast action seems to work best. In order to do this, everyone must know what to do and when. This takes practice.

chapter 11

GYMNASTIC BALANCING

O ur concern in this chapter is with individual balancing without apparatus, partner balancing, and balancing stunts on a chair. Many of these stunts are also used for pyramids (see Chapter 12). For our purposes here we will consider group balancing stunts with three or more performers as being pyramids.

Balancing acts have long been popular in circuses. These have taken many forms and often have been combined with other skills. For example, balancing stunts are frequently used in tumbling acts.

After learning the skills in this chapter, entertaining partner acts can be worked up.

EQUIPMENT

A five feet by ten feet tumbling mat at least two inches thick should be used. A sturdy non-folding chair can be used for the chair stunts. The chair can be painted in bright colors to give it a circus appearance.

Standard gym and recreational clothing is worn, except that the performers should either be barefooted or wear gymnastic shoes.

112

MECHANICS

Maintaining balance involves keeping the center of gravity over the base of support. It is easier to keep the body's center of gravity over a large base than a small one. For this reason, a headstand with a tripod base is easier to hold than a handstand.

In individual balancing stunts such as a handstand, corrections in balance are made by adjustments in the position of the body. For partner stunts it's generally best if the top performer remains a rigid object and lets the bottom man do the balancing. There are a few exceptions to this which will be pointed out with the stunts as they occur. The main principle to follow, however, is that as the balanced person starts to fall, the balancer should move the base of support back under the center of gravity. Of course, an individual balanced in a handstand can move the base of support by walking on the hands, but this is generally thought to be bad form when a handstand is being attempted. After all, walking on the hands is another stunt in which balance in motion is involved.

Balancing stunts can be learned at the same time as tumbling (see Chapter 10). The balancing stunts included here are arranged in order of difficulty. It's recommended that this order be followed and that each stunt be learned well before going on to the next one. In any case, the individual balancing should be learned before attempting the more difficult stunts with a partner.

Always begin with a warm up. The sequence shown in Chapter 3 can be used.

BASIC SKILLS

Individual Balancing

These stunts should be practiced on a tumbling mat. For some of the stunts you will need a spotter to assist.

Squat Head Balance

Assume a squat stand with the hands placed on the mat as shown. Notice that the hands are flat on the mat with the fingers forward. The knees are outside the arms. Lean forward and place head on mat. Raise toes slowly off mat and hold balance. Come down by first placing toes on mat.

A large three-point base is important. The hands should be some distance behind the head and about shoulder width apart. All motions should be done slowly. Jerky actions should be avoided.

If the forward roll in tumbling has been learned, a forward roll from the squat head balance can be attempted. This makes a neat finish.

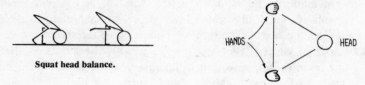

Squat head balance.

A large three point base is important.

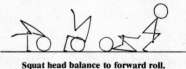

Squat head balance to forward roll.

Squat Hand Balance

Assume a squat stand with legs outside arms. This time the balance is on two points. Rock slowly forward until feet are off mat. Keep head up. Use finger pressure to keep from overbalancing. To come down, lower toes to mat.

A combination stunt that can now be attempted is to go from a squat head balance to a squat hand balance. To do this slowly take head from mat and rock back into support position on arms. The action should be done slowly in order to catch balance in squat hand balance.

Another variation is to go from the squat hand balance to the squat head balance. This should be done slowly and with control. Lower the head to the mat by bending arms slightly.

Also try a squat head balance, shift to squat hand balance, hold, back to squat head balance again, hold, then do forward roll out. This sequence effectively combines balancing and tumbling.

Headstand

Have a partner assist you as shown. Begin headstand by assuming a squat stand with legs together and hands flat on mat with fingers for-

Squat hand balance.

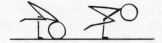

Squat head balance to squat hand balance.

Kick to headstand with partner assist.

Squat head balance, press up to headstand.

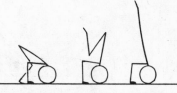

Tuck press up to headstand with knees together.

ward. Hands should be slightly more than shoulder width apart. Place one leg back, as shown. With partner standing close to catch ankles, kick up to headstand. When the position is correct there is no pike in the body. Extend toes toward ceiling. The body should be extended. A slight arch in the body is okay. However, too much arch is undesirable. It makes balancing more difficult and does not look as good.

Common difficulties are not assuming a three-point base with the hands apart and well back from head and kicking too vigorously into the headstand position.

Practice with the helper until balance can be maintained without assistance. However, have spotter stand by in case of overbalancing.

Next try starting from a squat head balance and pressing slowly into a headstand. Use a spotter on the first attempts. Come back down by returning slowly to the squat head balance. Have spotter step out of way and then, without feet touching mat, do forward roll.

This can now be used for a recovery in case of overbalancing. Before doing the forward roll, tuck first, as was done in returning to the squat head balance. However, with practice this can be done with the knees together and using only a partial tuck.

Next try a tuck press to a headstand with the knees together. In order to do this, the hips should be well over the head so that the center of gravity will be over the base of support.

Now for a more difficult one, a straddle press to headstand. Assume the starting position, as shown. Begin by raising hips first. Then slowly bring legs to straddle headstand. Legs then come together to regular headstand position. This one may take a little practice, so don't be discouraged if you can't make it on the first attempts. If extreme difficulties are encountered, go on to the next stunt and come back to this later.

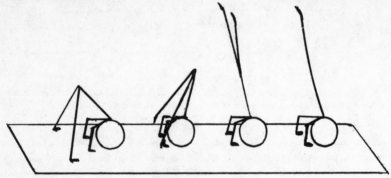

Straddle press up to headstand.

Headstand with Folded Arms

Begin by assuming a squat stance with legs together. Place head and folded arms on mat, as illustrated. Place one leg back. Kick slowly into headstand with folded arms. Balance is slightly more difficult than in doing a regular headstand, as the area of the base is reduced. In case of overbalancing, tuck and then do forward roll.

Head and Elbows Balance

Assume the same starting position as used for going into headstand with folded arms, except the hands are placed on head, as shown. Kick into head and elbows balance. This time the base is even smaller, so balance is more difficult. Recover from overbalancing involves doing tuck and then forward roll.

Forearm Balance

This time the head is off the mat. Assume the starting position shown. The elbows should be about shoulder width apart and the hands nearly touching each other. A partner can be positioned to assist in case of overbalancing. Make a smooth easy kick into the forearm balance. The body should be arched slightly.

A forward roll recovery from overbalancing can also be done. To do this, first place head on mat. Tuck before doing the roll.

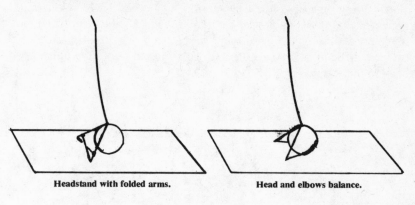

Headstand with folded arms.   Head and elbows balance.

Forearm balance.

Handstand

This has long been a popular stunt. For the first attempts, a mat is placed against a wall. Two spotters, positioned as shown, are also used. The starting position is about a foot away from the wall with the hands, which should be about shoulder width apart. The hands are flat and the fingers toward the wall. The head should be up with the eyes focused on the wall. Do *not* duck head. Keep looking at wall. This is extremely important. With the arms locked straight, kick into arched position with bottoms of feet against wall. Notice that only feet should be against wall. Hips are arched away from wall. Extend the body as high as possible, stretching the toes toward the ceiling. Hold balance for about ten seconds, then come back down to one foot.

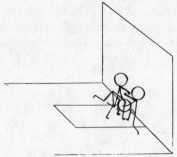

Position of spotters for handstand against wall.

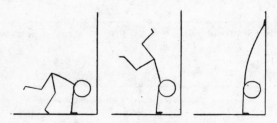

Kick up to handstand against wall.

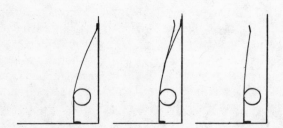

Practicing handstand by taking feet away from wall.

Practice this many times until the correct position can be assumed without help from the spotters.

The next step is to do a handstand with feet against wall and then pull feet one at a time slowly away from wall to regular handstand. To do this, move one foot a few inches from wall. Then slowly take other foot from wall and place it beside first foot. If balance is lost,

Kicking up to handstand with partner assist.

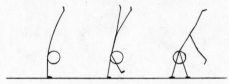

Handstand, cartwheel recovery from overbalancing.

Handstand, forward roll recovery from overbalancing.

either go back to position with feet against wall or come down to one foot. Remember to keep the head looking up at wall.

Practice this skill until a handstand can be held free of the wall. Learn to control the balance by applying finger pressure for overbalancing and bending arms slightly for underbalancing. After regaining balance, straighten arms again as soon as possible. Bent arms on a handstand is considered bad form and thus should be avoided as much as possible. Also try to maintain balance without moving the base of support, i.e., walking on hands. This is a separate stunt which should be learned only after the stationary handstand has been mastered.

The next step is to do a handstand on the mat in the open with a partner holding legs as shown. Then have partner give assistance only in case of overbalancing.

The next step is to learn to recover from overbalancing by stepping forward with one hand and doing a cartwheel out. For this, the cartwheel should first be learned (see Chapter 10). Begin by kicking to a handstand and deliberately overbalancing. Step forward with hand and cartwheel out to feet. Practice this action until it becomes automatic. Then kick into handstand and try to hold balance. If bal-

Jump tuck to handstand.   Squat hand balance, press up to handstand.

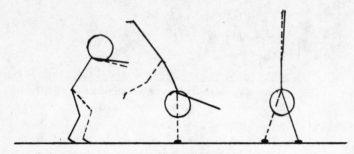

Cartwheel to handstand.

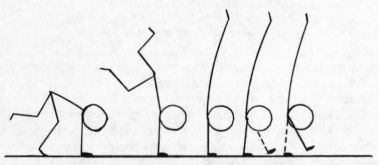

Kick up to handstand, walk forward on hands.

ance is lost back toward direction of kick-up, come back down on one foot. If balance is lost forward, step and cartwheel out.

Another method of recovery from overbalancing is to do a forward roll. To do this, tuck body and lower slowly to forward roll.

Of the two recoveries, the cartwheel out is more useful, as it can be used when doing handstands in places other than on a flat mat. For example, it can be used on the end of parallel bars and on a box.

Practice a handstand on the mat in the open until it can be done consistently. If more than one person is learning the handstand at the same time, have contests to see who can hold it the longest.

Another way to get into a handstand is to start with the feet together in a squat stance and jump tuck to the handstand, keeping the feet and knees side-by-side.

A slow press from a squat hand balance is another possibility. This is quite difficult, so you may want to go on and come back to this later.

Still another way to get into a handstand is to cartwheel into it. This amounts to doing half a cartwheel, stopping in the handstand position. The difficulty here is in stopping at the balance point. This may require a lot of practice.

Walking on Hands

After learning a good handstand, walking on the hands is generally easy. Begin by kicking to a handstand. Overbalance slightly and begin walking forward on hands. The principle is to keep moving the base of support (the hands) under the center of gravity.

This can be done on the floor as well as the mat. To recover from overbalancing, cartwheel out to feet. Use a set distance as a goal. At first this might be five feet. After this has been made, try for ten feet. Continue to work for longer distances until at least fifty feet can be covered. Also try walking in circles and backwards (toward the direction of the feet in the kick-up to the handstand).

A novelty number that always seems to go over well in a circus show is to have a race with the contestants walking on their hands. This can be between two lines or, if in a gym, the length of the floor.

Partner Balancing

In most cases it's not necessary for the "bottom" person to know how to hold the balance positions. For most of the stunts it makes things easier if the much heavier person is on the bottom.

Chest Balance

Assume the starting position as shown. Kick up into the chest balance. Hold. Then come back down on one foot first. On the initial attempts a spotter can be used to push the person back in case of overbalancing.

Swan on Partner's Feet

Begin in hand-holding position, as shown. Bottom person straightens legs and top person assumes swan position with back arched, head up, and arms out. Hold hands and dismount in reverse of mount.

Chest balance.   Swan on partner's feet.

Thigh stand from sitting on partner's shoulders.   Alternate method of getting into thigh stand.

Thigh Stand

An easy method to get into this is sitting on shoulders with top mounter's feet on partner's thighs. Bottom person holds top mounter's legs just above knees. Bottom person leans back as top person straightens knees and arches back. Arms should be out to side. Dismount can be the reverse of mounting. Also try coming down by having top mounter jump forward to feet on signal. Bottom person assists by catching his hips on way down.

Another way to get into the thigh stand is for top mounter to stand in front of bottom person, as shown. Bottom person lifts top mounter by hips as top mounter steps first one leg, then the other, up into position. Bottom person switches hands one at a time from hips to just above the knees.

Knee and Shoulder Balance

Start as shown. Notice that top person's arms are straight. They should remain extended throughout the stunt. Top mounter then kicks to knee and shoulder balance. Hold. Then come back down on one foot first.

Another method of getting into the knee and shoulder balance is a straddle press up, as shown. With the starting position shown, top mounter presses to knee and shoulder balance in straddle leg position. Legs are then brought together. The mechanics are similar to the straddle press up to a headstand, described above.

Kick up to knee and shoulder balance.

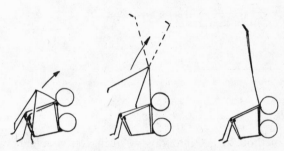

Straddle press up to knee and shoulder balance.

Foot-to-Hand Balance

Assume starting position, as shown. Top mounter pushes on partner's feet to help partner straighten arms into position. Top mounter releases hold on feet and stands up straight. Bottom person does the balancing. Top person should remain erect and look straight forward. If the top person tries to maintain balance by changing body positions, it will only make things more difficult. Bottom person should have feet extended while the balance position is held. To dismount, bottom person brings legs up again and top person is lowered to mat in reverse of mount.

Sitting on Partner's Shoulders

This is generally an easy stunt. Starting position is as shown. Bottom person then stands up. Top mounter hooks feet behind partner's back and sits up straight with arms out to side. Bottom person can also put arms out to sides.

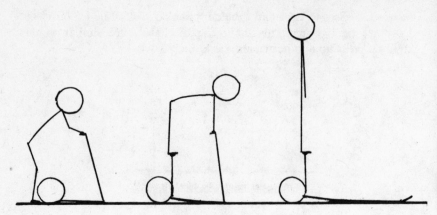

Foot-to-hand balance.

Sitting on partner's shoulders.

Dismount can be the reverse of getting up, or switch from sitting on shoulders to thigh stand, as was done previously.

Standing on Partner's Shoulders

Start by sitting on partner's shoulders, as described above. Join hands. Top mounter then places one foot on partner's shoulder and then the other foot on opposite shoulder. Top mounter then stands, releasing first one hand, then the other. In turn bottom person grasps first one, then the other, lower leg of top mounter. Top mounter can extend hands out to sides.

To dismount, hold hands again. Top mounter then jumps off forward to both feet.

Another method for getting into the standing position is shown. This is a little more difficult, but it presents a neater appearance.

Sitting to standing on partner's shoulders.

Alternate method of getting to partner's shoulders.

Arm-to-Arm

Assume the starting position shown. Top mounter then kicks to arm-to-arm balance. On the first attempts, use a spotter to push the top mounter back in case of overbalancing. To come back down, top mounter comes down on one leg first, then the other. This must be done to the bottom person's side.

Chair Balancing

Balancing Handstand on Chair

Use a spotter to assist in case of overbalancing. Assume the starting position shown. Kick up to handstand position. Keep head up. Extend body toward ceiling with feet together and toes pointed. Come back down to one foot first.

Press Up from Sitting to Handstand on Chair

This one is fairly difficult. Sit on chair as shown. Press to handstand. It is easiest if legs are in tuck position on the way up. Hold handstand. Come back down in reverse manner to sitting position.

BASIC ACTS

Balancing stunts can be worked into a tumbling act (see Chapter 10). An individual balancing act with the stunts described in this chapter is difficult to do effectively. A partner act generally works much better. The following is a suggested basic pattern for a partner act:

1. Chest balance.
2. Swan on partner's feet.
3. Thigh stand, switch to sitting on partner's shoulders, then standing, and dismount forward.
4. Knee and shoulder balance.
5. Foot-to-hand balance.
6. One person walks across stage on hands.
7. One person does handstand on chair—if possible, a press up from sitting.
8. Arm-to-arm balance.

If done smoothly, this act can be quite effective. Only a basic outline is given. It will take considerable planning to work out the positions and between-stunt sequences.

Kick up to arm-to-arm balance.

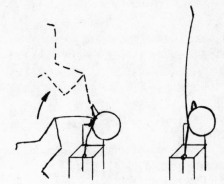

Kick up to handstand on chair.

Press up from straddle sitting to handstand on chair.

chapter 12

FORMING PYRAMIDS

Pyramid building makes for an exciting act in amateur circus shows. Beginners and skilled performers can work together. The act can be all male, all female, or mixed. Since a large group can perform together, it makes an ideal act for use just before intermission or as a finale.

Drawings depicting pyramids were made in ancient Egypt. In the modern circus pyramids are used in various forms in many acts. Four-high column and five-high with two or three in the base-levels pyramids have been performed. A backward somersault has been done from a teeter board to the top of a three, two, one, one, four-high pyramid, making a five-high.

Our main concern here will be with the straight line pyramids that are symmetrical and more or less triangular shaped. The pyramids described are done without apparatus. However, these can easily be adapted for use with apparatus such as parallel bars and tables, as the basic skills are the same. Pyramids can also be done on ladders (see Chapter 17).

EQUIPMENT

The only special equipment needed is a gymnastic mat from about twenty to thirty feet long, depending on the size of the pyramids to be performed.

For shows it would be best if the performers all wear the same costumes. Gymnastic shoes should be worn, as these look neat and have soft soles for standing on shoulders and so on. For more information about costumes, see Chapter 22.

MECHANICS

The mechanics are basically the same as those given in Chapter 11, only this time they apply to larger groups.

Here are some basic principles for performing group pyramids:

1. The base should be sound. Use the heaviest and strongest performers to support the greatest load.

2. Use the lightest performers on top.

3. Each person should know exactly what to do.

4. Make sure each person can perform his or her part with control and confidence.

5. Simplicity in design generally results in the best pyramids.

6. Building, holding, dismounting, and changing from one pyramid to the next should be done smoothly and following a set pattern.

Cues should be called out by one person, who may or may not be in the act as part of the pyramids. The following is a suggested sequence for calling out the cues by numbers:

1. From a straight line facing the audience with the tallest person in the center and tapering at each end to the shortest, the bottom group takes positions.

2. Other performers take positions ready for mounting.

3. Everyone mounts to pyramid positions.

4. Hold with everyone in position.

5. Dismount and return to original straight line.

Before each pyramid the same person can call out the next pyramid. However, the routines should be practiced to the point where only a quick cue will be needed.

BASIC SKILLS

The pyramids shown in this chapter can be considered as samples of the hundreds of possibilities. It's recommended that each group design their own pyramids. The basic principle is to have one grouping as a centerpiece and then placing an end grouping on each side to make a symmetrical pattern.

The balancing stunts described in Chapter 11 are the basic skills needed by some of the performers and form basic one and two person parts for larger pyramids.

Three Persons

A number of three-person symmetrical pyramids are shown. These have been arranged in order of increasing difficulty. These can be done individually or as centerpeices for large-group pyramids.

Non-symmetrical arrangements that can be used individually or as edge pieces for larger pyramids are shown.

Four Persons

Here are some ideas for four-person arrangements. The symmetrical patterns can be used as centerpieces and the non-symmetrical ones as edge pieces.

Five Persons

Here are some of the possibilities for five persons. Notice that some of these are built in two steps, that is, the bottom layer, a middle layer, and a top layer or balance position such as a handstand.

Six-Person Three-Two-One Standing

This makes an ideal ending for a tumbling act (see Chapter 10). While six persons are used in the actual pyramid, it helps to have one additional person to help the top mounter up.

Begin by positioning bottom layer. Middle layer then mounts. An easy way for the top person to get up is to stand on another person's shoulders behind the two layer formation and then mount. The final step is for the top person to stand up. Hold position for about six to eight seconds. Top mounter then dismounts by holding arms of layer below and jumping down forward. Middle performers slow the fall. Next layer dismounts in the same manner.

With practice this pyramid can be formed quickly. After holding, the dismounting should be done smoothly. For this pyramid it's important that each layer consist of lighter performers.

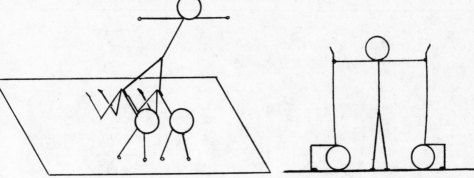

Three person symmetrical pyramid.

Three person symmetrical pyramid.

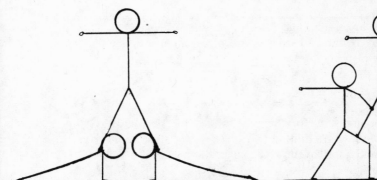

Three person symmetrical pyramid.

Three person symmetrical pyramid.

Three person symmetrical pyramid.

Three person symmetrical pyramid.

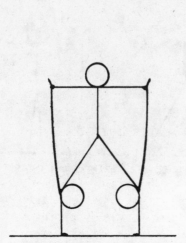

Three person symmetrical pyramid.

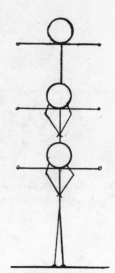

Three person symmetrical pyramid.

Three person non-symmetrical pyramid.

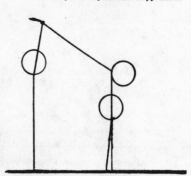

Three person non-symmetrical pyramid.

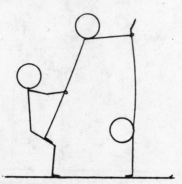

Three person non-symmetrical pyramid.

Three person non-symmetrical pyramid.

Six person three-two-one standing pyramid.

LARGE-GROUP PYRAMIDS

This section will also be used as the basic act for this chapter. Sample large-group pyramids are shown. These can be adapted for various levels of skill and numbers of performers. Organization should be by both size and skill. The best performers should be used for the more difficult parts, such as handstands. There are a number of places where beginners can be used along with experienced performers.

Another consideration for an amateur act is how many pyramids to do. With a large group, from four to six seems to work out best. This is generally better than doing a larger number where similar patterns will be repeated and may possibly bore the audience. As a general rule, the act should end with the audience still wanting to see more.

The pyramids described have been based on a straight line. However, using the same basic principles, acts can be formed using circular, triangular, and other patterns. For example, three separate identical group pyramids can be grouped together with each formation making up one side of a triangle. Walking pyramids are still another possibility.

Four person symmetrical pyramid.

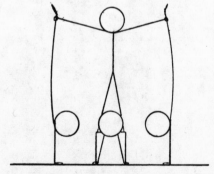

Four person symmetrical pyramid.

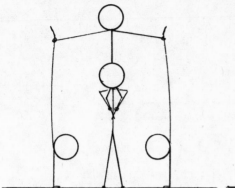

Four person symmetrical pyramid.

Four person non-symmetrical pyramid.

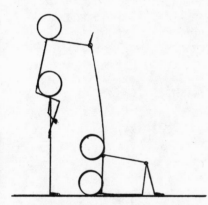

Four person non-symmetrical pyramid.

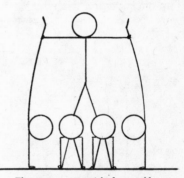

Five person symmetrical pyramid.

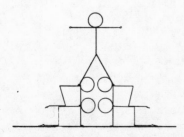

Five person symmetrical pyramid.

Five person symmetrical pyramid.

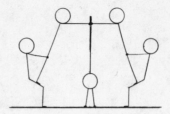

Five person symmetrical pyramid.

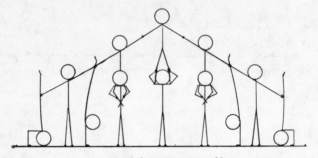

Sample large group pryamid.

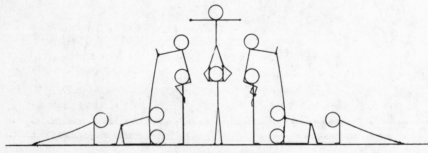

Sample large group pyramid.

Sample large group pyramid.

chapter 13

TRAMPOLINING

The trampoline, as it is known today, is a rather recent innovation. Exactly who invented the trampoline remains controversial. One was used, however, by a professional act, "The Walloons," in 1910. Trampolining has continued to be a popular circus act. It is also a competitive sport.

Perhaps the most difficult trampolining feat that has ever been performed is four consecutive triple backward somersaults without any extra bounces between them! The feat was done by Len Ranson of Australia in 1970. Other extremely difficult feats include a triple twisting double back somersault, done by Wayne Miller of the United States, and a five and one-half twisting back somersault, accomplished by Judy Wills of the United States.

Trampolining is a fun activity. After learning the basic skills in this chapter, you can work up both individual and group trampoline acts. The trampoline is also ideal for clown routines. But first comes the basic skills.

Trampolining—author competing in gymnastic competition for Southern Illinois University in 1959.

EQUIPMENT

Ideal is a regulation competitive trampoline, which has a bed of woven webbing about twelve feet long and eight feet wide. Smaller trampolines can also be used. The bed can be of canvas or webbing and attached to the frame by elastic cords or metal springs. The frame should be covered with safety pads.

Regular gym or recreational clothing and soft-soled gymnastic shoes are most suitable for trampolining, but for performing in shows special costumes are desirable (see Chapter 22).

MECHANICS

Many different mechanical principles are involved in trampolining. These will be covered when they are needed.

Safety is an important consideration. Here are some basic rules:

1. Have spotters around the edge of the trampoline to assist if you start to go off the edge.

2. Start with the easiest skills first. Learn each one before going on to the next one.

3. Always warm-up before trampolining. A suggested sequence is given in Chapter 3.

4. Trampolining is not for everyone. A reasonable level of agility and physical fitness is essential. While almost all ages, both men and women, have taken up trampolining, extreme caution is advised for anyone past college age.

5. Concentrate on what you are doing.

6. After learning the basic stunts detailed in this chapter, you may want to go on to more advanced ones. For this, an experienced trampoline coach is recommended.

7. Although it's not absolutely essential, it will make things easier if the basic tumbling stunts covered in Chapter 10 are learned first.

BASIC SKILLS

Individual Stunts

Even though these are individual stunts, it's best to have five learning at the same time. This way there will always be four spotters, one on each side of the trampoline, and rest periods between turns.

Mounting and Dismounting

Although there are stunts that can be performed when mounting and dismounting from a trampoline, they are not for the beginner. For the time being, mount by holding the frame and climbing up to the trampoline. Dismount in the same manner; that is, stop bouncing, reach down and grab the edge of the trampoline frame, and climb down slowly.

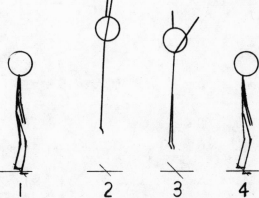

Basic trampoline bouncing.

Bouncing

This may not be a stunt, but it's basic to everything on the trampoline. Begin by standing in the center of the bed with your feet about shoulder width apart. Try easy bouncing. Then try to add the following mechanics. Arms should be at sides when contact with bed is made. Arms swing forward and up as you bounce into the air. At peak of flight arms are above head. On descent, arms are swung downward to sides. Feet come together in the air and apart again for contact with bed.

To stop bouncing, the knees are flexed as contact with the bed is made. This "absorbs" the spring. Practice this until it can be done well. When control is lost, bouncing can be quickly stopped in this manner.

Tuck Bounce.

With regular bouncing, bring knees up into a tuck position, holding shins in hands. Release tuck and continue regular bouncing.

Half-twist

With regular bouncing, make one-half turn to face opposite end of trampoline and continue bouncing. The twist is initiated by swinging right arm across chest on take-off from bed to twist to the left, and the left arm across chest to twist to the right.

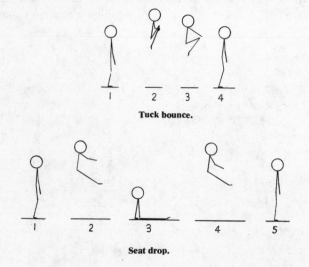

Tuck bounce.

Seat drop.

Seat Drop

Begin by sitting down on bed and assuming correct landing position with legs extended, toes pointed forward, and hands at sides with fingers pointed toward feet. Come to stand.

Next stand in center of bed. With no preliminary bouncing, jump up and raise legs forward, leaning backward slightly as you do so. Land in seat drop position, as previously practiced. Try to bounce back up to feet.

The next step is to try it from two or three easy bounces. After the seat drop, return to feet. After this can be done with control, try a seat drop, return to feet, and seat drop again with no extra bounces between them. This is called "swing time." Next try three seat drops in swing time.

Seat Drop, Half-twist to Seat Drop

This stunt is often called a "swivel hips." This describes the main action of the stunt. Basically the stunt is to do a seat drop, swing legs under body with half-turn to second seat drop, and bounce up feet.

Here's how to work up to it. Do a regular seat drop, except execute a half-twist from the sitting position to the feet. Try this a number of times.

Next do the same motion, except this time swing legs through without the feet touching the bed to a second seat drop. Bounce to stand. When done correctly the legs swing directly under the body, not around to the side.

Back Drop

Begin from a stand. Bend head forward and place chin on chest. Arch back as shown. At the instant balance is lost, raise legs off bed. This must be done without diving backwards. Try to return to feet.

Next, get down on hands and knees, as shown. Bounce up and down on hands and knees. Then pull legs forward and under body to back drop position. Bounce up to stand.

Do not throw your head backwards when you do this. Keep chin down against chest. The stunt should be done in one spot, without traveling backwards.

Each time assume the hands and knees position without bouncing or dropping into it. Start the bouncing after the position has been assumed. When this can be done through to a controlled back drop,

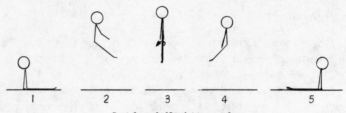

Seat drop, half twist to seat drop.

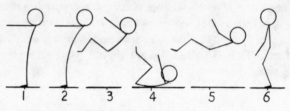

Back drop from arch stand.

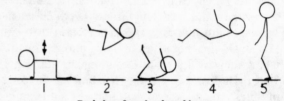

Back drop from hands and knees.

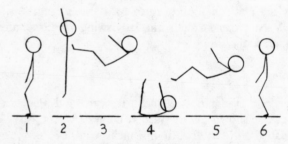

Back drop from bouncing.

Front drop from hands and knees.

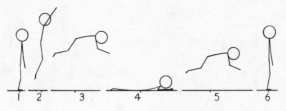

Front drop from bouncing.

then try starting from the feet, first with low bouncing, then finally from regular bouncing. When done correctly the landing on the back and the take-off and return to feet will all be in approximately the same spot. The legs should be extended when the back drop is made.

Front Drop

Begin by getting down on hands and knees in the center of the bed. Bounce up and down on hands and knees. Drop to front, as shown. Return immediately to hands and knees. Notice that the legs are extended back. Do not dive forward. Notice also that a slight hip bend is maintained. Do not shoot the legs back into a deep arch.

When this can be done with control, try starting from a stand. Without bouncing first, do a front drop and return to feet. Remember not to dive forward and also to maintain a slight bend in the hips. The take-off and return to the feet should be in approximately the same spot.

Next try a front drop from low bouncing. Gradually work up to regular bouncing.

Front drops can now be done in swing time. After the return to feet from one front drop, do second front drop. Then try three in a row.

Front Drop, Tuck Through to Seat Drop

Do a regular front drop, except push off more vigorously with hands and tuck all the way through to a seat drop.

Half-twist to Front Drop

Start from a stand. Look over one shoulder. Without bouncing first, jump into front drop with half-twist from feet. This is fairly easy, since the eyes are focused in the direction of the landing.

Gradually work up to the point where the half-twist to front drop can be done from regular bouncing.

Seat Drop, Full Twist to Seat Drop

Begin by getting down in a sitting position. Then start bouncing up and down a few inches in the sitting position. With the feet remaining in one spot, do full turn to a second seat drop position. The important part is leaving the feet in one spot. Think of it as rolling around the toes in the air.

After this can be done with control, start from low bouncing. Do regular seat drop, then full twist to second seat drop before returning to feet.

Half-turntable

Do front drop. Push sideways with hands. Tuck as body turns. When half-turn has been completed, open out into second front drop. Bounce back up to the feet. The turn is sideways and the head and feet remain at approximately the same level.

Combinations

At this point stunts can be combined. For example, try a front drop, tuck through to seat drop, half-twist to seat drop (swivel hips), and return to feet. Or start the same sequence with a half-twist to front drop. Hundreds of combinations are possible.

Also try doing combinations of stunts with no extra bounces (swing time). For example, try a seat drop, feet, back drop, feet, front drop, feet, half-twist to front drop, and return to feet.

Combining stunts adds to the effect of a trampoline act.

Specialty Stunts

With Hoop

Use a plastic hula hoop. While bouncing, try circling hoop over body. This can be done from head to feet and from feet to head. Learn both ways.

Learn to do a seat drop with only one hand on the bed while holding the hoop in the other hand. Then, without returning to feet, try to do two seat drops. Next do the same stunt, only as the body leaves the bed after the first seat drop, circle the hoop over the body from feet to head.

Many other similar hoop stunts are possible. Also, try to work up a sequence of stunts with the hoop.

Jumping Rope

Using a standard jumping rope with swivel handles, try rope jumping with regular bouncing. Double and triple spins of the rope, both forward and backwards, should be possible. Also try crossing hands while jumping.

By doing seat drops without hands, you can jump rope at the same time. For example, begin by jumping rope with regular bouncing. Continue spinning rope while doing one or more seat drops in swing time or two or more seat drops without returning to feet between them.

Another possibility is to have two helpers spin a long rope while bouncing and stunts are performed on the trampoline. By using a prearranged sequence, the helpers can better control the rope spinning.

Partner Stunts

Both performers should be able to do the individual stunts before trying these. With the two performers positioned on the trampoline as shown, begin alternating bounces. One performer should be at the peak of flight when the other leaves the bed, and so on. It's best if one performer makes the corrections in timing, while the other person continues with even bouncing.

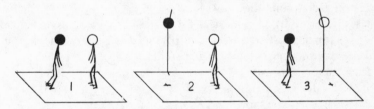

Basic alternate bouncing for partner stunts.

Using this pattern, the individual stunts can be performed. The performers can work facing each other about four feet apart and to the side of the bed. The sequence of stunts to be performed should be prearranged. For example, the sequence might be seat drop, feet, back drop, feet, front drop, feet. Many combinations are possible.

Another stunt is for both performers to be on the centerline of the trampoline about four feet apart. One performer then does a seat drop with straddled legs, while the other one does a regular seat drop.

BASIC ACTS

Since many combinations are possible, only skeletons for acts are given here. To these originality should be added.

One Person

For this act helpers, who can also serve as spotters, will be needed. Keep each part of act short.

1. Mount trampoline and do combinations of basic skills, starting with the easiest stunts first. Do *not* include your best routine at this point.
2. Hoop stunts.
3. Second sequence of basic skills. These should be more difficult than first sequence, but still not the best routine.
4. Sequence with regular jumping rope.
5. Routine of most difficult stunts.
6. With two helpers spinning long rope, do routine.

Group Act

Since only one or two people will be performing at a time it's best not to have more than four or five in the act unless more than one trampoline is used, in which case there can be four or five on each trampoline with the acts done at the same time. The acts can be different on each trampoline, however.

Use the same basic pattern as for a one-person act, except divide the parts up instead of having one person doing the whole act, and add one or two sequences of partner stunts at appropriate places.

Important points are:

1. Keep the act moving.
2. Keep each part short.
3. Build in difficulty for dramatic effect.
4. Finish with the audience still wanting more.

chapter 14

FOR YOUNGSTERS

SEVEN TO ELEVEN—

STUNTS ON THE

ROLLED MAT

While all ages can do stunts on a rolled mat, it's especially suitable for boys and girls from about seven to eleven years old. With some adult help, this age group can put together an exciting act in short time.

EQUIPMENT

Standard gym mats are used. One or more mats are rolled tightly together to form a roll about two and one-half feet in diameter. The rolled mat is then placed crossways in the center of a twenty-foot long mat, which should be at least four inches thick. This can be made up of more than one mat. All mats should be at least five feet wide.

Regular gym or recreational clothing is preferable, except gymnastic shoes should be used or else the performers should be barefoot.

MECHANICS

Mechanics of vaulting and tumbling are both involved. The forward and backward rolls should be learned (see Chapter 10) before

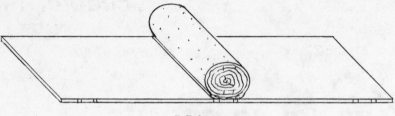

Rolled mat.

starting rolled mat skills. Warm up first. The sequence given in Chapter 3 is suitable.

Rolled mat skills can be taught to a group of children in Follow the Leader fashion. One older person can provide the necessary spotting.

BASIC SKILLS

The basic approach for most of the skills is a fast run started about thirty feet back from the rolled mat. A few of the stunts are done from a stand at the rolled mat. For these a walking approach to the mat can be used.

One-Foot Leap from Top

Run, one-foot take-off, other foot steps on top of rolled mat, leap, land on original take-off foot, and continue running.

Hurdle

Run, hurdle over rolled mat, and continue running. Basically, it's a giant step over the mat.

Two-Foot Leap from Top

Run, one-foot take-off, land on both feet on top of rolled mat, leap, and land on both feet. Make the leap as high as possible.

Two-Foot Leap from Top, Forward Roll

This is the same, except *after* landing on two feet, do a forward roll. This is *not* a forward roll from the top of the mat. On the first attempts pause between the landing on two feet and the forward roll.

Two-Foot Leap from Top with Half-twist

Run, one-foot take-off, land on both feet on top of rolled mat, leap with half-twist, and land on both feet. Make the leap as high as possible.

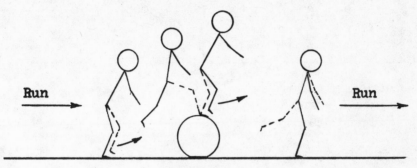

One-foot leap from top.

Two-Foot Leap from Top with Half-twist, Backward Roll

This is the same, except *after* landing from the leap with half-twist, do a backward roll. On the first attempts make a definite pause between landing on both feet and the backward roll.

Side Vault Right

Run, two-foot take-off, place both hands on top of rolled mat about shoulder width apart, and vault with body passing over rolled mat to performer's right. When going over the rolled mat, the right side of the body should be in a down position. Land on two feet facing forward in the direction of the start.

Side Vault Left

This is the same, except the side vault is to the left. Again, end facing the same way as at the start.

Squat to Feet, Leap from Top

Run, two-foot take-off, place both hands on top of rolled mat shoulder width apart, and squat to feet between arms with knees together. Stand and leap. Land on both feet.

Hurdle.

Two-foot leap from top.

Two-foot leap from top with half twist.

Side vault.

Squat vault.

Forward roll over.

One-foot takeoff to seat drop.

Squat Vault

On this vault the feet do not contact the top of the rolled mat. Run, two-foot take-off, place both hands on top of rolled mat shoulder width apart, and squat between arms, pushing off vigorously with hands. Land on both feet. A spotter can assist on the initial attempts.

Forward Roll Over

This looks much more difficult than it actually is. One or two spotters can assist on the first attempts. Start from squat stand in front of rolled mat. This is the basic forward roll position (see Chapter 10). Head must be placed as close to rolled mat as possible. Do forward roll over rolled mat. Always start from standstill. Do *not* use a running approach.

One-Foot Take-Off to Seat Drop

Take-off is from one-foot as far back from rolled mat as possible. Land sitting on rolled mat with hands placed at sides. A common mistake is to take-off too close to the rolled mat.

BASIC ACT

The act is done in a crossing pattern. Two lines are used, as shown. The approach for each line should be about thirty feet. Each line should have the same number of performers. This act works well with up to about 24 performers, twelve in each line.

The first person in each line leads each new stunt, which each person does one time. After each stunt, line up in the other line. The stunts are done crossing, with two performers doing the same stunt at the same time. When person ahead reaches take-off mat, next person starts run.

The following stunts are done in the crossing pattern:
1. One-foot leap from top.
2. Hurdle.
3. Two-foot leap from top, forward roll.
4. Two-foot leap from top with half-twist, backward roll.
5. Side vault right (legs pass outward from center of rolled mat).
6. Squat to feet, leap from top.
7. Squat vault.
8. Forward roll over.
9. One-foot take-off to seat drop.

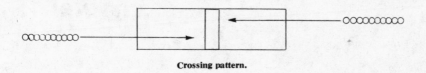

Crossing pattern.

It will take some practice to get the timing so that two performers do the stunts at the same time. It's helpful if one of the two persons at the front of the lines (at the start) begin the run, while the other person uses this as the cue to begin. The rest of the performers begin just as the person ahead reaches the take-off mat. For the forward roll over the rolled mat, a walking approach should be used by all performers.

chapter 15

MINI-TRAMPOLINE AND

GYM SPRINGBOARD STUNTS

The same skills can be done on both mini-trampolines and gym springboards. Both are suitable for amateur circus acts.

By running down a long inclined platform and springing from a flexible board, Billy Pape, a professional circus performer in the 1920s, was reported to have done a forward somersault over five elephants and two camels which were lined up side-by-side.

The mini-trampoline is a relatively new invention, at least in its modern form. It probably developed as an offshoot from the regular trampoline.

EQUIPMENT

A standard gym springboard is used. Manufactured models are readily available.

A number of companies make mini-trampolines. For the stunts in this chapter the mini-trampoline should be permanently fixed or adjustable to an inclined position, as shown.

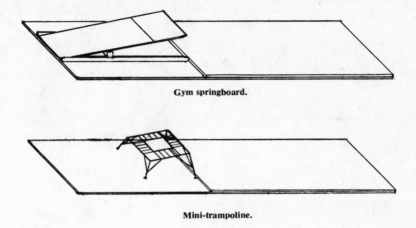

Gym springboard.

Mini-trampoline.

Soft landing mats are needed. These can be made up of one or more mats to at least a four-inch thickness. The landing mat should be at least ten feet long and five feet wide. A thick foam-filled mat can also be used.

Regular gym and recreational clothing are worn, except that gymnastic shoes should be used.

MECHANICS

The same basic run and hurdle, as shown, is used for both the mini-trampoline and gym springboard. In both cases the run is changed into forward and upward motion. Generally a slow run is used on the springboard, while the approach to the mini-trampoline can be quite fast.

Mechanics for individual stunts will be covered as they are needed.

After learning the basic skills in this chapter, many people want to go on to more advanced ones. For this an experienced coach is recommended.

A number of performers can learn these skills as a group in Follow the Leader fashion. On the initial attempts at each new stunt, it's a good idea to have two spotters positioned as shown, except for the straddle jump, where the spotters would be in the way.

All stunts should first be done from a slow approach and easy jump. Control is the most important factor in the beginning stages. For some of the skills forward and backward rolls are required (see Chapter 10 for techniques).

Approach to springboard.   Approach to mini-trampoline.

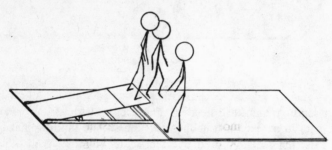

On the initial attempts at each new stunt, it's a good idea to use spotters.

BASIC SKILLS

Follow the same progression on either apparatus. A somewhat slower approach should be used for the springboard. Don't forget to use spotters on the first attempts at each new stunt.

Straight Jump

Jump upward and forward. The landing is on two feet with the knees slightly flexed.

Straight Jump, Forward Roll

This is the same as above, except after landing on feet, do forward roll. On the first attempts pause between landing on feet and the forward roll. Gradually shorten the pause.

Jump with Half-twist

This is the same as the straight jump, except a half-twist is performed before the landing on the feet. Work for control.

Jump with Half-twist, Backward Roll

This is the same as above, except a backward roll is done after landing on two feet. On the initial attempts pause before starting the roll.

Tuck Jump

This is the same as the straight jump, except a tuck position with hands on shins is assumed while in the air. Open out for the landing. Do not lean foward or backwards from the jump. The body should be upright while in the air.

Pike Jump

This is the same, except that a pike position is used. *(Note:* In diving and gymnastics, the pike position is one in which the hips are bent, knees are straight, the head is pressed forward and the hands touch the toes or clasp the legs behind and just above the knees.)

Swan Jump

An arched body position is assumed in the air. Pike slightly prior to landing.

Straddle Jump

Don't use the spotters for this one, as they would be in the way. This is the same as the pike jump, except the legs are apart. The feet come together again just before landing.

Jump with Full Twist

This is similar to the jump with half-twist, except this time a full twist is performed before landing. It's important to jump with the body in a vertical position without leaning forward or backwards. Control is important here.

Jump with Full Twist, Forward Roll

This is the same, except after the landing from the full twist, do a forward roll. On the first attempts pause between landing on the feet and the forward roll.

Straight jump.   Jump with half twist.

Tuck jump.   Pike Jump.

BASIC ACT

Mini-trampoline and springboard acts work well with from six to twelve performers. The same pattern can be used for both the mini-trampoline and springboard. The performers work from a single line in Follow the Leader fashion. Each person does each stunt one time. When the person ahead starts hurdle, the next person begins the run. This will keep the act moving.

The following is a suggested order of stunts:

Swan jump.   Jump with full twist.

1. Straight jump.
2. Straight jump, forward roll.
3. Jump with half-twist, backward roll.
4. Tuck jump.
5. Pike jump.
6. Swan jump.
7. Straddle jump
8. Jump with full twist, forward roll.

chapter 16

VAULTING

There are many forms of vaulting. Our concern here is with side horse (without pommels) vaulting, using a reuther board as a take-off platform. In this manner basic vaulting can be learned by both boys and girls and, within limits, men and women. After college age, considerable discretion should be used.

After a number of performers have learned the basic vaults, an entertaining act can be worked up.

EQUIPMENT

A side horse adjusted to a low height without pommels is ideal for learning. Other possibilities are a vaulting box, an elephant (a mat over parallel bars), or a buck (similar to a side horse except only a couple of feet from end to end).

The recommended take-off platform is a reuther board, which is the standard gymnastic take-off board used for vaulting in the Olympics. Other possibilities if a reuther board is not available are mini-trampolines and gym springboards.

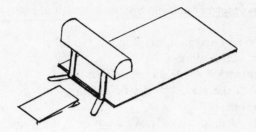

Basic vaulting setup.

Run

Takeoff from reuther board.

The landing mat should be at least five feet wide and ten feet long. A larger mat is even better. The mat should be at least four inches thick. This can be built up in layers. If available, a thick sponge-filled mat is ideal.

Many schools, YMCAs, and recreation centers have the necessary equipment for vaulting. Here we'll assume that you will be using a reuther board, a side horse without pommel (they can be detached from most side horses), and a soft landing mat. This same setup can be used for amateur acts with a group of performers.

MECHANICS

Vaulting involves changing the forward momentum of a run into forward and upward motion. The hands contact the horse while in the air from the jump, and various body positions are performed before, during, and after the hands contact the horse.

The approach to the take-off board should be a controlled run. From one foot come down on the board on both feet, as was done in performing the diving roll in tumbling. Focus the eyes on the horse where the hands will be placed.

This basic approach will be used for all of the vaults covered in this chapter.

Spotting, which can be defined as assisting another person,

becomes important in vaulting. Spotting techniques will be explained as needed.

Here are some important things to keep in mind:

1. Never practice alone.

2. Concentrate on what you are doing.

3. Start with the easiest vaults first. Learn each one before going on to the next one.

4. Always warmup for at least fifteen minutes before doing actual vaulting. The sequence outlined in Chapter 3 can be used.

5. Begin with the horse at a low height. Place the take-off board about a foot from the horse. The height of the horse can gradually be increased as the vaulting skill improves. The board can also be moved further from the horse, increasing the flight from take-off to hand contact.

6. It's best to wear gymnastic shoes with non-slippery soles. Tennis shoes and other stiff-soled shoes make for awkward vaulting. Barefooted vaulting is not a good idea, as there is considerable danger of stubbing toes and so on.

7. For both sexes standard gym and recreational clothing can be worn. Special costumes can be worn for an amateur act (see Chapter 22).

8. After learning the basic vaulting detailed in this chapter, you may want to go on to more advanced skills. For this, an experienced vaulting coach is highly recommended.

BASIC SKILLS

For each vault the same approach run and take-off is used, as detailed above. A thirty-foot run is about right for learning the basic vaults. The reuther board should be about a foot from the center of the near side of the horse as the vaulter stands facing it. The landing mat should be placed right against the far side of the horse.

On the initial attempts of each new vault, one or two spotters should be used. The number and position is given for each vault. The spotter(s) should assist the vaulter only as needed.

Squat to Feet, Jump to Stand

From take-off, place hands on top of horse shoulder width apart and squat to feet between arms with knees together. Spotter stands as shown and assists performer by upper arms. Vaulter then extends

One spotter.

Two spotters.

body to stand and jumps to stand on landing mat. Spotter backs up quickly during this phase.

Two spotters, positioned as shown, can also be used.

Practice this vault many times before going on. *It's basic to everything that follows.*

Squat to Feet, Jump to Stand, Forward Roll

Use two spotters, positioned as shown. Before attempting this vault, the performer should be able to do a good forward roll (see Chapter 10). Do the same vault as before, except this time *after landing on feet,* do a forward roll. On the first attempts, pause in a standing position before starting the forward roll. After confidence and control is gained, the vault can be done without assistance from the spotters. However, it's a good idea to have the spotters in position, just in case.

Squat to Feet, Jump to Stand with Half-twist

Use two spotters positioned the same as previously. Start as on the previous two vaults, except the jump from the horse to the mat is done with a half-twist. They may take considerable practice before a controlled landing can be made.

Squat to Feet, Jump to Stand with Half-twist, Backward Roll

Use two spotters. Do the same vault as above, except this time after landing on feet, do a backward roll. Before attempting this the performer should be able to do a good backward roll (see Chapter 10).

On the first attempts, pause in a standing position before starting the backward roll. The length of the pause is gradually reduced, but be sure to land on feet before starting the roll.

Squat Vault

On this stunt the feet do not contact the top of the horse. Use two spotters on the initial attempts. From take-off, place hands on top of horse shoulder width apart and squat between arms, pushing off with hands. Land in a standing position with the knees slightly flexed.

Side Vault

This vault can be done either to the right or left. It should be learned both ways. Use one spotter. The spotter stands on the side opposite to the leg direction. This is important, as otherwise the spotter will not be able to get out of the way of the vaulter's legs.

From take-off, place hands on top of horse shoulder width apart. Body passes over horse with side in down position. Landing is facing straight forward. The body should be extended sideways when passing over the horse.

Learn both directions before going on to the next vault.

Front Vault

The spotting is the same as for the side vault. This vault starts the same way, except this time the performer's body faces the horse and the landing is sideways. The body should be extended during the flight over the horse. One hand remains on the horse for the landing. Learn both directions.

Rear Vault

The spotting technique is the same. This time the back of the body is toward the horse. Hold a pike position (bent hips with the legs straight) when passing over the horse. The landing is sideways, opposite to the direction of the front vault. Learn both directions before going on to next stunt.

Wolf Vault

One spotter is used on the side opposite to that of the performer's outward extended leg. From take-off, place hands on top of horse shoulder width apart. Inside leg is in a squat position and outside leg is outward and extended. The landing is straight forward with the feet close together. Learn both directions.

Straddle to Feet, Jump to Stand

This time one spotter is used. The spotter stands at the center of the horse and assists the performer by the upper arms. During the jump, the spotter must back up quickly.

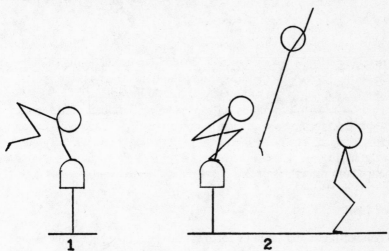

1   **2**

Squat to feet, jump to stand.

Squat to feet, jump to stand with half twist.

Squat vault.

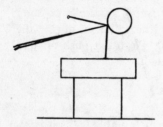

Side vault.

Front vault.

Rear vault.

Straddle vault.

Wolf vault.

From take-off, place hands on top of horse shoulder width apart and straddle to top of horse. Stand and jump, bringing feet together before landing.

After learning this with control, a forward roll can be done *after* landing on feet. On the initial attempts, pause before doing the roll.

The jump to stand can also be done with a half-twist. Finally, a backward roll can be added to this. Again, pause on the initial attempts.

Straddle Vault

One spotter is used in the center of the horse, as was done for the straddle to feet, jump to stand. This time the performer pushes off with the hands and the legs pass over the horse in a straddle position without touching the horse. The legs should be extended during the straddle. Bring legs together before landing. A strong push-off and longer flight before landing makes a better vault.

BASIC ACT

An effective individual act would be extremely unlikely, as it is almost impossible to keep the act moving. Our concern here will be with a group act. This can be very effective with from about six to twelve vaulters. The vaulters start from a single line. After each vault, circle back and join the end of the line. The lead vaulter starts off with the next vault each time he comes to the front of the line. Each vaulter starts the run when the vaulter ahead takes off from the reuther board. This will keep the act moving, yet allow the vaulter ahead to be out of the way of the next person.

The act can be done in strict, formal-gymnastic style, but an informal act generally works better. The performers have more fun, and the audience will probably enjoy it more.

The following sequence can be used with all vaulters doing each vault one time through. If desired, the act can be shortened by eliminating some of the vaults.

1. Squat to feet, jump to stand, forward roll.
2. Squat to feet, jump to stand with half-twist, backward roll.
3. Squat vault.
3. Side vault with legs to right.
5. Side vault with legs to left.
6. Front vault with legs to right.
7. Front vault with legs to left.

8. Rear vault with legs to right.
9. Rear vault with legs to left.
10. Wolf vault with extended leg to right.
11. Wolf vault with extended leg to left.
12. Straddle to feet, jump to stand, forward roll.
13. Straddle to feet, jump to stand with half-twist, backward roll.
14. Straddle vault.

chapter 17

LADDER SPECTACULARS

Two ladders make an ideal platform for building pyramids. This type of act is often called "Roman ladders." Ladder acts look much more difficult than they actually are. It looks as though the ladders are delicately balanced when in fact they are quite stable. Both beginners and skilled performers can work together. Since a large group is involved, this is a good act to use as a finale in an amateur circus show.

EQUIPMENT

Standard wooden ladders that are about two feet wide with bolts or rods running through round rungs are ideal. These can be purchased by the foot at lumber yards. A matching pair about twelve feet tall is about right for working up an act, although taller ladders have been used. It is this writer's opinion, however, that artistic skill is much more important than trying to see how high above the ground something can be done.

The twelve-foot ladder can have twelve rungs. A thirteenth rung is added three inches from the top as shown in the diagram. These should be padded with foam rubber and covered with a material such as coarse canvas that will provide firm footing. The metal crosspieces should be through bolted with two bolts on each end. This is important, as the crosspieces must not turn.

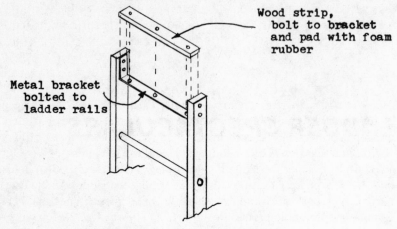

Wood strip, bolt to bracket and pad with foam rubber

Metal bracket bolted to ladder rails

Special rung added three inches from top of ladder.

Rubber pads should be attached to the bottoms of the ladders. The ladders can be painted as desired, except that the rungs should be left unfinished.

A gymnastic mat long enough to extend under both ladders is used. The ladders will be placed approximately four and a half feet apart. A ten-foot long mat will give space for the performers on each side. However, if ground pyramids are to be performed at the sides, a longer mat should be used. This can be made up of more than one mat. However, the mat that extends under both ladders should be in one piece.

MECHANICS

Balance is quite stable, as there is a fairly large four-point base. If the ladders start to fall to one side with performers in the center, correction is easily made by shifting weight to ladder on side opposite direction of falling, and pulling other ladder back.

With a number of performers on the sides of the ladders, they should be matched approximately in weight and perform the same stunts at the same time. In this way the ladders will each support ap-

proximately the same weight, making it possible for the center performers to control the balance of the ladders easily.

The width of the base will depend on the size of the center performers. With the ladders vertical to the ground, the center performers should be able to hold the adjacent rungs comfortably with the
arms extended to the sides. They should also be able to straddle their
legs to this width, but this is generally quite easy to do. Once the
width is determined, it should be marked on the mat so that the
ladders can be quickly placed.

BASIC SKILLS

Two or three performers are generally used to control the balance
of the ladders when twelve-foot ladders are used. With taller ladders
more performers can be used in this manner. The control performers
should practice alone before adding side and top mounters.

Begin by placing the ladders in position. One performer then holds
both ladders and climbs upward while keeping the ladders in balance.
Next center performer follows, then the third person goes up. Performers stop climbing when positioned as shown. Use this arrangement for now. For a ladder act, you may want to vary this somewhat.

With the center performers positioned as shown, practice letting
ladders start to fall to one side and then bringing ladders back into
balance. The center performers must learn to work together to do
this. They should look straight forward rather than down. Control of
the ladders is largely by feel.

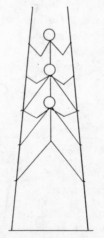

Basic stationary pattern.

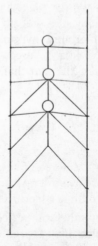

Basic spread pattern.

This is the basic stationary pattern. The second pattern is the spread formation. To do this the center performers extend arms outward on signal. The position is held. Then on signal the ladders are brought back in.

The center performers come down in reverse order of climbing up. The ladders can be caught and lowered by other performers in the act or, in shows, a stage crew. The details of this need to be worked out for each particular situation.

Practice with just the three center performers until the positions can be quickly assumed and the ladders easily controlled. The other performers can then be added. Side performers climb opposite each other and at the same time. When a single top person is used, the climb is up the center of the ladders.

Stationary Formations

Suggested stationary formations (without spreading ladders apart) are shown. A highly skilled performer should be used for standing and doing shoulder stand on top of ladders. This person should also practice climbing up to the top in the center of the ladders behind the regular center persons.

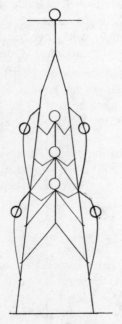

Stationary formation.

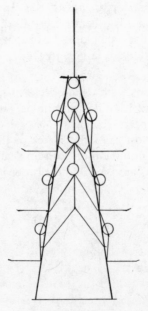

Stationary formation.

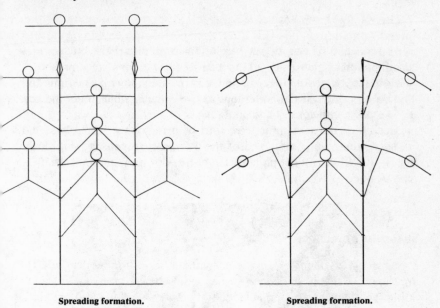

Spreading formation.   Spreading formation.

Someone is needed to call out the cues. It is best if this person is not one of the performers on the ladders. For the stationary formations, the center performers climb and take positions first. A cue is then given for the other performers to climb and take positions. If a single top mounter is used, the climb is between the ladders at the same time as the side performers are going up. The next signal is to pyramid positions and hold. The hold position should be for about eight or ten seconds.

In most cases the switch to the next formation should be possible with a minimum of position switching. This will depend on what formations are used and the order in which they are presented. The cues might be, "Take positions, ready, now."

Spreading Formations

The spreading formations are done in the same way, except there is an extra step. The ladders are spread apart, the position held, and then the ladders are brought back in again.

Suggested spreading formations are shown. These should be considered only as samples, as there are hundreds of possibilities.

BASIC ACT

A sequence of five or six formations seems to work out well. A combination of stationary and spreading formations is recommended. The sequence should be planned and written down. Then the act should be practiced until everyone knows exactly what to do and can do the parts with control and confidence.

Each time the act is practiced, start by bringing the ladders out and standing them up. At the end of the act, practice getting them down again. It will take some practice to get this down to the point where it can be done smoothly.

Stationary formation.

Special costumes greatly add to the effect of this act. All performers should wear gymnastic shoes. The cues should be kept simple. These can be by numbers or words.

Keep the act moving. Hold each formation for about eight seconds, just long enough to show it, and then go on to the next one. The act should be short enough that it will end with the audience still wanting to see more.

The ladder formations can be combined with ground pyramids. This will involve a larger group. An end piece (see Chapter 12) can be used on each side of the ladders.

The ladder formations can also be done with the ladders on top of a large table. For this a sturdy table should be used as it must provide a firm foundation for the ladders. Blocks with cutouts for the ladder feet are bolted to the top of the table. By painting the top of the table and the blocks black, the audience probably won't be able to see the cutouts.

The ladder formations can then be performed in the same way as without the table. The table should be on a solid floor rather than on top of a mat.

chapter 18

CROWD PLEASERS ON

THE HORIZONTAL BAR

There have been many professional horizontal bar acts. Many of these use two or three bars, performing stunts from one bar to another. The horizontal bar is also popular in amateur circuses and is a competitive event in gymnastic competition, including the Olympics.

Many amazing stunts have been performed on and from the horizontal bar. One of the most difficult is the triple flyaway to ground (release bar on forward swing, three backward somersaults before landing on feet), which has been performed by both amateurs and professionals.

Horizontal bars are found in many playgrounds, and many good performers have started here. While the horizontal bar has mainly been of interest to boys and men, there have also been good female performers. It is interesting to note that many of the top performers on playground bars in elementary schools are girls.

The basic skills covered in this chapter are done on a single bar at chest level. With these skills individual and team acts can be performed.

EQUIPMENT

Standard gymnastic horizontal bars that can be adjusted to shoulder level are ideal. The bar should be at least six feet wide and eight feet is even better. These are generally mounted with floor attachments. Models are now available with independent suspension systems, which are ideal for use in shows where floor mounting plates are not available.

Also needed is gymnastic chalk, which is available at sporting good stores. This is used on the hands for a secure grip. Gymnastic handgrips are also a good idea, as they allow longer workouts without sore hands. These can also be purchased at sporting goods stores.

MECHANICS

Three grips are used on the horizontal bar: the regular grip, the reverse grip, and the mixed grip. The grip used depends on the stunt that is being performed. For swinging forward, the regular grip provides the most secure hold. The reverse grip is best for swinging backwards.

Mechanics will be explained as needed along with the individual stunts. Safety is an important consideration. Here are some basic rules:

1. Make sure the equipment is properly set up. Thick mats should be used; these should extend about ten feet or more away from the center of the bar in both directions.

2. For learning new stunts, use spotters.

3. Do not practice when you're alone.

4. Concentrate on what you are doing.

5. Always use chalk on hands. It should be pointed out that a special gymnastic chalk is used. The chalk used for writing on boards is *not* suitable.

6. Learn stunts in a step-by-step manner, starting with the easiest ones. Learn each one before going on to the next.

7. After learning the basic stunts in this chapter with the bar at shoulder height, you may want to go on to a higher bar and more advanced stunts. For this an experienced horizontal bar coach is recommended.

8. Always warm up before starting on the bar. The sequence given in Chapter 3 is suggested.

BASIC SKILLS

The horizontal bar should be at chest or shoulder height. Clean the bar. Fine sandpaper can be used for this. After warm-up you are ready to begin on the bar. Apply chalk to your hands.

Skin the Cat

Use a regular grip. Bring legs up in tuck position between arms. Extend slowly through to position shown. Bring legs back again to mat. One or two spotters can be used on the first attempts.

Skin the cat.

Front Pull-over

Use a regular grip. Stand as shown. Jump off both feet, keeping arms bent. Pike and pull hips up and over the bar. Straighten up to front support with extended arms and body.

One or two spotters should be used on the initial attempts, positioned as shown. Their purpose is to give only minimum assistance, not to lift the performer over the bar so that he thinks he is doing the stunt.

Front pull-over.

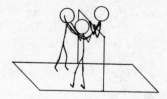

Spotting technique for front pull-over.

Single-knee Kip

Do skin the cat and hook one leg, as shown. The other leg should be straight. Swing back and forth by kicking straight leg down and back. On back of swing pull body forward over bar. To dismount, lower body back to knee hang below bar and disengage hooked leg.

On the single-knee kip it's important to keep the bottom leg straight. This will promote the necessary momentum from the leg swing to complete the stunt.

Backward Single-knee Circle

Begin by doing single-knee kip. Then, with back leg straight, push upper body up and back. Begin circle from as high as possible. Circle around bar and end in original starting position.

After learning to do one hip circle, try two in a row. After completing the first circle, repeat the same action for the second one.

Bar-snap Dismount

Stand as shown. Use a regular grip. Jump up behind bar, bring knees up into pike position, and snap outward, releasing grip. Land on both feet with knees slightly bent and arms out.

For learning, spotters should be used as shown. Start with low jump and easy snap. Gradually work up to higher jump and body snap.

Also try the bar-snap dismount from a front support. Do a front pull-over to get in the starting position. Then drop back in pike position and do bar-snap dismount to feet. Use spotters on the first attempts.

Forward Single-knee Circle

Begin with single-knee kip. In support position with one leg over bar, change hands to reverse grip. Push shoulders as high upward above bar as possible and circle forward. At bottom of circle the single-knee kip position is assumed, and the finish is the same as for the single-knee kip. The lower leg should be kept straight.

After learning to do one forward single-knee circle, try two in a row, which should be only a little more difficult than doing one. Also try three and four in a row.

Single-knee kip.

Backward single-knee circle.

Bar-snap dismount.

Forward single-knee circle.

Backward Pull-over

Start with skin the cat. Hook knees over bar. Extend body and arch back. Pull upward with arms. End with sitting position on bar.

Knee-swing Dismount

Start with skin the cat. Hook knees over bar. Reach forward with arms to start swing. Build swing. At the peak of the forward swing, straighten knees and dismount to feet landing with knees bent slightly.

The spotting method is shown. It's important that the performer not release knee hold until the peak of the forward swing. This point should be stressed. On the first attempts a spotter can call out the timing.

After this has been learned, try starting from a sitting position on top of the bar. Fall backwards, hooking knees. Swing from knees and straighten knees at forward peak of swing for dismount. The same spotting technique should be used.

Another variation of the knee-swing dismount is to start from a stationary knee-hang position. Reach upward and forward with arms, releasing knee hold at the same time. Dismount to feet. Use a spotter on the first attempts.

Backward Hip Circle

Start by doing front pull-over to front support. Bend forward slightly at hips. Cast body back into slight arch. As body falls back to bar, circle legs under bar. The ending is essentially the same as a front pull-over. The hips should be held close to the bar during the hip circle.

After one backward hip circle, a second one can follow, as the ending and starting position for the stunt are the same.

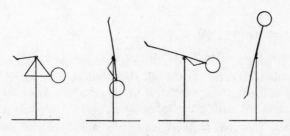

Backward pull-over.

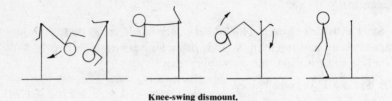

Knee-swing dismount.

Spotting technique for knee-swing dismount.   Backward hip circle.

Backward Double-knee Circle

Begin by doing backward pull-over. From sitting on bar, push upward and back with shoulders. As body starts backwards, hook knees. Circle backwards around bar to sitting position on bar.

After learning one backward double-knee circle, two or three in a row should not be much more difficult.

Forward Hip Circle

Start by doing front pull-over to front support. Keep head up and push body up as high as possible. Fall forward, keeping body straight until horizontal with floor. Pike quickly and continue around bar to front-support position. During the circle, the body should be held to the bar.

Forward Double-knee Circle

Begin by doing backward pull-over. In sitting position on bar, switch hands to reverse grip. Push shoulders upward as high as possible. Circle forward. Knees hook the bar at bottom of circle. Continue circle until sitting on top of bar.

After one forward double-knee circle, a second one can follow. Repeat the same action. Also try three and four times in a row.

Tap Kip

Start as shown. Jump up and back, piking the body slightly. Legs glide forward and tap mat. Quickly bring legs to bar. Hold legs to bar, then kip upward. End in front-support position.

The timing is extremely important in this stunt. The tap must be far forward. The legs must then be brought quickly to the bar. Delay slightly with legs held close to bar before the vigorous kip action.

Backward double-knee circle.   Forward hip circle.

Forward double-knee circle.

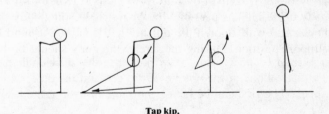

Tap kip.

Combinations

Many of the above skills can be done in combinations. For example, do a front pull-over, backward hip circle, and end with a bar-snap dismount. Or do a tap kip, forward hip circle, and end with a bar-snap dismount. Many other similar combinations can also be done. Try to use combinations where one stunt will flow smoothly into the next one.

BASIC ACTS

An individual act is difficult, as it is hard to keep moving. However, it can be done. Here's one possible individual act.

The act consists of three combination routines of five or six stunts each. These should be arranged in order of difficulty and each should end with a dismount. After each sequence, take a brief rest, then continue with the next sequence. The last sequence should be the most difficult.

An act with two or more performers is easier to keep moving, as rest is possible when someone else is performing. Also, the additional performers make it possible for those in the act to spot each other.

If two performers are used, each can do three short sequences, one after the other. If three performers, each person can do two sequences.

An interesting addition for group acts is to have two performers on the bar at the same time. One way to do this is to have both persons facing the same direction, about a foot and a half apart. The horizontal bar should be eight feet wide for this. In this position, the two performers do the same combination of stunts in a synchronized pattern. This will take considerable practice, but the effect is well worth the effort.

Another method is for the performers to face opposite directions on the bar, with a foot and a half distance between them. Combinations of stunts are again done in a synchronized pattern, only in opposite directions. In order to do this, each person must know the routine. A good way to get the timing is to first practice facing in the same direction.

The partner sequences can be worked into the individual combinations by placing one at the middle of the act, and the other at the end for a finale. The first can be facing the same direction; the last facing opposite ways.

chapter 19

TRAPEZE SKILLS

Various forms of trapeze have long been popular circus acts. Perhaps the most spectacular of all circus skills is the flying trapeze, where the performer does stunts from one trapeze bar to the hands of a catcher on another bar. Triple flyaways (release bar at forward peak of swing and execute three backward somersaults) have been performed in this manner. It should be pointed out however that a number of present acts are announcing triple somersaults, but only doing doubles. The audience seldom knows the difference, but this writer feels that this type of deceit does considerable harm to the image of the circus and is unfair to those who have done or can do this stunt.

The cost of the rigging and the fact that even the simplest flying trapeze skill is quite difficult precludes the topic's coverage here. However, the individual stationary and swinging trapeze detailed here is fun and challenging, and the basic skills to be learned here are the foundation for all types of trapeze work. After learning basic skills, an exciting individual trapeze act can be performed.

EQUIPMENT

A horizontal bar about two feet long and an inch in diameter is suspended from two ropes. The ends of the bar and the ropes near the attachments to the bar should be padded. Trapeze bars complete with rope and padding can be purchased from gymnastic supply houses.

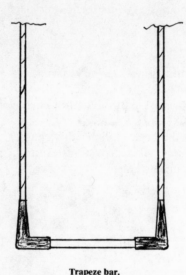

Trapeze bar.

Attachments for connecting these to ceiling beams are also available. The setup must be strong and well mounted.

If possible the height of the bar should be adjustable. Two heights for each performer are recommended: chest high and just above the point where the performer can touch the mat when hanging with body and legs fully extended.

A gymnastic mat should be placed below the trapeze. For the stationary trapeze the mat should be at least ten feet long and five feet wide. For swinging work, the mat should extend well past the bar at peaks of swing. A minimum thickness of four inches of mat is recommended.

The performer should wear gymnastic shoes and use gymnastic chalk on the hands. For catching by the ankles and toes, heavy wool socks can be worn with the shoes.

MECHANICS

Many of the mechanics are the same as for the horizontal bar, and it's highly recommended that the basic skills be learned on the horizontal bar before attempting them on the trapeze bar. There are two important reasons for this: the trapeze presents a less stable, and thus generally more difficult, apparatus, and trapeze work is more difficult to spot, especially when swinging.

Here are some important points for learning stationary and swinging trapeze skills:

1. Always warm up first. The sequence in Chapter 3 can be used.
2. Never practice alone.
3. Always concentrate on what you're doing.
4. Use gymnastic chalk on your hands.
5. Start with the easiest skills and learn each one before going on to the next stunt.
6. After learning the basic skills in this chapter, you may want to continue on with more advanced stunts. For this, an experienced trapeze coach is recommended.

BASIC SKILLS

Stationary Trapeze

Many of the stunts can be done with the trapeze bar at chest height. A few require the bar at a height where the feet cannot touch the ground when hanging with body fully extended.

Skin the Cat

Use a regular grip (see Chapter 18 for a discussion on this). Bring legs up in tuck position between arms and under trapeze bar. Extend through to position shown. Then bring legs back through arms again to mat.

Bird's Nest

Begin with skin the cat and hook toes. Arch body through to form bird's nest. Head should be up and feet and legs together. To come down, reverse action.

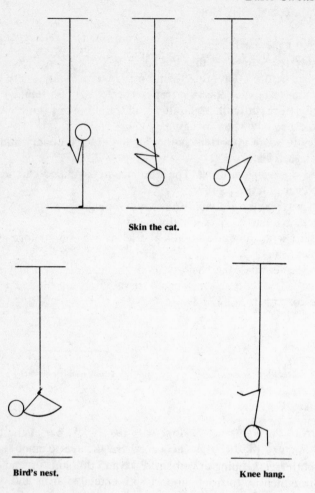

Skin the cat.

Bird's nest.   Knee hang.

Knee Hang

Begin with skin the cat and hook knees over bar. Release grip on bar and drop down to knee hang. Come back up by piking body and regrasping bar. Unhook legs and come down forward to feet.

Horizontal Leg Hook Hang

Do skin the cat and hook one leg over bar. Keeping hand grip on bar, assume horizontal body position. Toes should be pointed and the head should be back.

Sitting Position on Bar

Do skin the cat and hook both legs over bar. Switch hand grip from bar to ropes. Pull body up to sitting position. Legs should be straight and toes pointed. Dismount by reversing mounting steps.

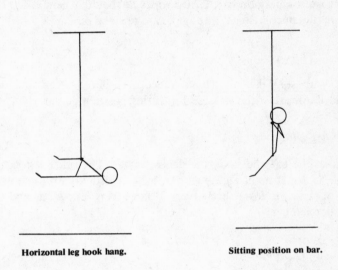

Horizontal leg hook hang.   Sitting position on bar.

Front Pull-over

Use a regular grip. With the bar at chest height a jump can be used. Jump off both feet, keeping arms bent. Pike and pull hips up and over the bar. Straighten up to front support with extended arms and body. Toes should be pointed.

The front pull-over is more difficult when the trapeze bar is at a height where the feet cannot touch the ground. To do this, start with chin-up, then pull legs over bar.

Front Support, Roll Forward

Begin with a front pull-over to front support. Then roll slowly forward to tuck hang and feet. If bar is up high, the roll is to hanging position. The stunt is essentially the reverse of the front pull over. The roll should be slow and the body tucked on the first attempts. With practice it can also be done in a pike position.

Stand on Bar

Begin by sitting on bar (described above). Grasp ropes above head. Pull upward and place feet on bar. Stand up. Reverse the procedure to get back down.

Skin the Cat on Ropes

Begin by standing on bar. Grasp ropes at shoulder height. Do skin the cat and then come back through again to stand on bar.

Backward Pull-over

Start with skin the cat. Hook knees over bar. Extend and arch body. Pull upward with arms. End in sitting position on bar.

Single-knee Kip

Do skin the cat and hook one leg over bar. The other leg is held straight. Swing straight leg down and back. Pull body up to support. To get back down, lower body back to knee hang below bar and disengage hooked leg.

Knee-swing Dismount

Start with skin the cat. Hook knees over bar. Reach forward with arms to start body swing. Build swing (of body, ropes should remain stationary). At peak of a forward swing, straighten knees and dismount. Land with knees slightly bent. Use two spotters on the first attempts.

Feet and Ankle Hang, Backwards

This is a basic position on the trapeze. Do skin the cat and hook feet as shown. Release hand grip and extend body to hanging position upside down. The bar must be up high for this. Tuck body and bring hands up to bar to get back down.

Knee Hang, Drop to Feet and Ankle Hang, Backwards

Begin by assuming knee hang position. Then straighten legs and force feet outward. Hook feet over ropes and end in feet and ankle hang, backwards.

Sitting Position on Bar, Fall Back to Feet
and Ankle Hang, Backwards

Assume sitting position on bar. Fall backwards. Force feet outward and hook feet over ropes. End in feet and ankle hang, backwards.

Feet and Ankle Hang, Forward

Begin with skin the cat. Hook feet over ropes in front of bar. Release hand grip and extend body to hanging position upside down. The bar must be up high for this. To get back down, tuck body and reach up and grasp bar.

Front Support, Fall Forward to Feet
and Ankle Hang, Forward

Assume front-support position on bar. Fall forward. Force feet outward and hook ropes. End in feet and ankle hang, forward.

Standing on bar.

Feet and ankle hang, backwards.

Foot Hang from Bar

Do skin the cat and hook feet over bar. Release hand grasp and slowly lower body to hanging position. The bar must be up high for this. Slowly tuck body up and regrasp bar. Spotters should be used on the first attempts.

Heel Hang from Bar

Again the bar must be up high. Begin by doing skin the cat. Hook heels. Slowly lower body to hanging position. To get back up, slowly tuck body and regrasp bar. Spotters should be used on the first attempts.

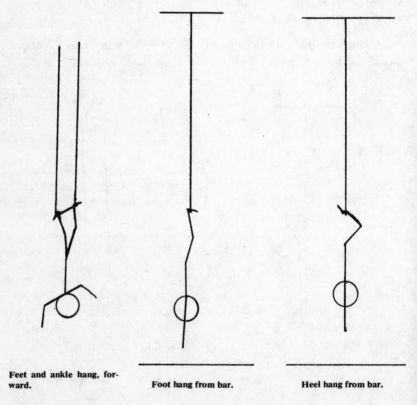

Feet and ankle hang, forward.   Foot hang from bar.   Heel hang from bar.

Combinations

Many combinations can now be attempted. The bar can be up high for these. Here's a sample: Skin the cat, bird's nest, knee hang, reach up and grasp ropes and pull to sitting position on bar, fall back to feet and ankle hang, backwards, reach up and grasp bar, disengage feet and bring them between arms. Hook knees over bar, knee hang, and knee-swing dismount.

Hundreds of similar combinations can be formed from the above described skills.

Swinging Trapeze

It's recommended that the stunts themselves first be mastered on the stationary trapeze. Swinging can be started in several ways: by sitting on the bar and swinging by pumping legs as is done on a playground swing, by having someone swing you by pushing, and by sitting on the trapeze bar and holding an adjacent rope, which someone swings.

The trapeze should be at a height where the feet cannot touch the ground when hanging from hands in extended position.

Sitting on Bar

Assume a sitting position on the stationary bar. Then start swinging. The technique is the same as on a playground swing.

Standing on Bar

Assume a standing position on the stationary bar. Then start swinging. The technique is the same as standing on a playground swing.

Hanging by Hands on Bar

Start swinging in sitting position. Grasp bar and slowly drop below bar with hooked knees. Disengage legs. Timing should be with legs forward at peak of forward swing. Finish by doing skin the cat, hooking legs over bar, switching hand grip to ropes, and pulling up to sitting position on bar.

Bird's Nest

While swinging with hang from hands on bar, do skin the cat. Hook toes over bar. Arch body through to form bird's nest. Head should be up and feet and legs together. To come down, reverse action.

The timing is generally easiest if the skin the cat is done at peak of forward swing. Have toes hooked by peak of back swing, at which time the arch through should be done. Come out of arch position at peak of next back swing.

Knee Hang

While swinging with hang from hands on bar, do skin the cat. Hook legs over bar. Release grip on bar and drop down slowly to knee hang. Come back up by bending forward at hips and regrasping bar. Disengage legs to hanging by hands on bar or with knees still over bar grasp ropes and pull to sitting position above bar.

The timing is generally easiest if skin the cat is done at peak of forward swing. Have legs hooked over bar by peak of back swing and lower to knee hang position at this point.

Feet and Ankle Hang, Backwards

While swinging with hang from hands on bar, do skin the cat and hook feet behind bar and over ropes. Release hand grip and extend body to hanging position upside down. Tuck body and bring hands up to bar to come out of stunt.

Knee Hang, Drop to Feet and Ankle Hang, Backwards

Assume knee hang while swinging. At peak of forward swing, straighten legs and force feet outward. Hook feet over ropes and end in feet and ankle hang.

The drop can also be made at the peak of the back swing.

Sitting Position on Bar, Fall Back to Feet and Ankle Hang, Backwards

With swing while sitting on bar, fall backwards at peak of forward swing. Force feet outward and hook feet over ropes. End in feet and ankle hang.

The drop can also be made at the peak of the back swing.

Front Pull-over

On peak of forward swing while hanging from hands on bar, do a front pull-over. The technique is the same as on the stationary trapeze, except now the timing of the swing becomes important. Hold front support above bar while swinging. On next peak of forward swing, roll forward to hanging from hands below bar. On the first attempts at the roll, use a tuck position to slow the roll so grip can be maintained.

Feet and Ankle Hang, Forward

While swinging with hang from hands on bar, do skin the cat. Hook feet over ropes in front of bar. Release hand grip and extend body to handing position upside down. To get back up, tuck body and reach up and grasp bar.

Front Support, Fall Forward to Feet and Ankle Hang, Forward

While swinging in front-support position, fall forward at peak of forward swing. Force feet outward and hook ropes in feet and ankle hang.

BASIC ACT

Although individual acts can be done on either the stationary or swinging trapeze, a combination is suggested. One possible act is to begin with a routine on the stationary trapeze. End with a knee swing dismount. Add chalk to hands and rest briefly. Then do second routine on stationary trapeze. End this time sitting on the bar. Take a short rest. Have helper toss chalk up. Add chalk to hands. Then do swinging routine. For this it looks better if the swing is started by holding an adjacent rope that is swung by a helper. Do a sequence of stunts on the swinging trapeze. In between more difficult stunts, use sitting and standing on bar for resting. At the end of the routine the adjacent rope can be used to slow and stop swing more rapidly. The timing for this should be worked out with helper.

The act should be kept short. Do easier tricks first. Build to more difficult stunts. End act with audience still wanting to see more.

chapter 20

CLOWNING

C lowns have been an important part of almost every successful circus. Clowning is not, however, for everyone. For success, natural ability is required. This is perhaps the most important ingredient. A person either has it or doesn't. With this natural gift there are a number of things that can be done to improve the clowning, such as skill, costumes and make-up, routines, and props, which is what this chapter is about.

SKILL

Many of the basic circus skills covered in other chapters of this book can also be used for clowning. In most cases it takes more skill to clown than to do a regular act. For example, to clown on a unicycle requires considerable riding skill. A common failure is for a clown to try to be funny about trying to ride a unicycle when in fact he cannot.

Here are some ways basic circus skills can be used in clowning:

1. In a tumbling act a clown can be the one to do the dive roll over the crash pyramid (see Chapter 10). A clown could come out

196

and push the regular performer out of the way, yelling, "I can do it, I can do it!" At this point the pyramid is built up and a dive roll over looks impossible. During the clown's approach run with big awkward steps, just before the take-off on the diving roll, the pyramid crashes.

2. A clown could come out in the middle of a juggling act, shouting that he wants to try it. After dropping all the balls a few times, a cascade pattern is done with a high and wide toss-out (see Chapter 4). A good way to finish is to announce an attempt to juggle twelve balls. Have the balls tied together. Drill a hole through each ball and run the string through them. Juggling twelve balls will now be easy.

3. Stilt walking skills offer a number of possibilities. For example, try a man and a woman clown dancing together on strap-on stilts. Clowns on stilts are also good in grand entry parades.

4. A wild clown on a unicycle out of control provides a good change of pace. To do this effectively, the clown must be quite skilled on the unicycle. Another possibility is to attempt an obstacle of plastic bottles just after a performer in a regular act has made it through. Only instead of making it through without hitting the bottles, knock all of them over.

5. During a balancing act, just after a regular performer has done a handstand, the clown comes out shouting, "I can stand on my hands!" Finally he is allowed to try. He puts his hands under his feet and stands on his hands.

6. During the ladder act with the center performers in position holding the ladders balanced, two clowns come out, one chasing the other. They chase each other up one side of the ladders, over the top, and down the other side. They run out of the performer's entrance-exit, with the chase still going on.

7. On the trapeze complete clown routines can be done by making use of the falling feet and ankle catches. The techniques needed are described in Chapter 19. The clown must be quite skilled to do this effectively, however.

8. For almost any of the basic acts, a clown mimicking stunt done by a serious performer can draw laughter.

9. Another possibility is to perform follow-the-leader stunts with a regular performer or a group of clowns. The clowns, of course, get the timing all wrong and bump into each other and so on.

10. Fake falling seems to be popular in clowning. This requires considerable skill but can be quite effective. The clown must be able to do these so that no actual injury occurs.

The comedy in the above stunts is mainly a matter of proficiency in basic circus skills. This is perhaps the easiest way for the beginning clown to elicit laughter from the audience, as it is mainly a stunt itself that is used to achieve the effect. However, clowning is an art that goes far beyond this. A clown is a very special kind of actor or actress. If successful, there will be laughter. For a clown to achieve this effect, it's important that he have an understanding of his audience.

Here are some of the things that constitute a funny situation:
1. Restraint and freedom from inhibition
2. Pretense
3. Make-believe
4. Exaggeration

Much of clowning is done with pantomime. It takes considerable skill to make gestures that will convey comedy. An artistic clown can depict primary emotions, such as sadness, happiness, joy and hate, by pantomime.

Much of the effect of successful clowning is the result of doing the unexpected. Clowning is based on violation of the logical and the use of the extreme. It also helps if the clown can show that he has ability at a skill after demonstrating his aptitude for the ridiculous. Whenever a gimmick is used to fool the audience, it's almost always effective to show the audience the method by which they were fooled. Examples of how this can be done are given later in this chapter.

ROUTINES AND PROPS

A number of routines along with the necessary props are given below. These can be used to keep the audience amused between acts and during intermission, or they can be used as full-fledged clown acts. The routines are intended only as suggestions. By all means add your own originality.

Balancing a Ball on Umbrella

A gimmick is used for this. A string is attached to the ball and the center of the umbrella, as shown. Fishing leader can be used to make it more difficult for the audience to see. Now when the umbrella is angled and rotated, the ball stays neatly balanced, rolling around the rim of the umbrella.

After demonstrating the skill, the clown then walks off, perhaps after folding umbrella, with the ball dangling from the string.

This is an example of showing the audience the method by which they were fooled. This has an unexpected element and almost always brings laughter.

The effect can be greatly improved by the clown's skill. Practice the routine in front of a mirror. Try to make it look like a skillful, legitimate balancing stunt. Build to the dramatic moment when the ball will be hanging from the string.

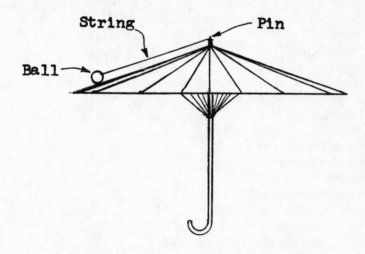

Balancing a ball on umbrella.

Pole Balancing

Connect a tray to the end of a wooden pole, as shown. Then fasten a large plastic pitcher and glasses to the tray with short lengths of string. Fill the pitcher and glasses with confetti.

The clown comes out with all items in place on the tray, holding the pole. The pole is then balanced from hand, chin, or forehead. But now the pole falls off balance over the audience. At the last instant, the clown catches the pole as the empty pitcher and glasses are hanging above the audience, the confetti having spilled all over them.

Before attempting this in an actual show, the clown should have considerable balancing experience. The pole should fall toward the audience with the clown running forward trying to restore its balance. The stop is made just before reaching audience.

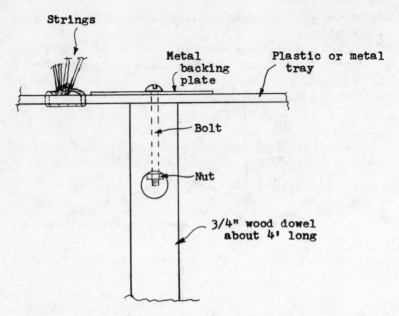

Equipment for pole balancing routine.

Water Pails

This is an old routine, but it never seems to fail. Start by having one clown chase another clown with a pail of water. Chaser catches up and throws pail of water over clown being chased. Wet clown runs and gets another pail, which is filled with confetti instead of water. The chasing positions are now reversed. Clown being chased falls down next to audience. Pail of confetti is thrown out over the audience.

This routine generally works best if done rapidly. Audience must be led to believe that the second pail will also contain water. Everything must build to the surprise of the confetti falling over the audience.

Rubber Tightwire

Construct the "tightwire" from a long band of rubber connected to two boxes. A clown can then perform great walking feats, as the band of rubber will be on the floor. A balancing pole will add to the effect. This act is ideal when programmed to follow right after the regular tightwire act.

Slapsticks

These can be constructed from three thin sheets of flexible wood, as shown. Bore a number of holes through the center sheet. Attach the sheets together at the handle. Routines can now be performed with two or more clowns. The slapsticks will make a loud noise whenever applied to another clown's posterior.

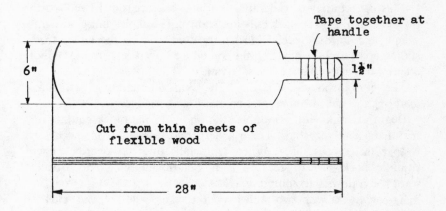

Construction of a slapstick.

Clown/Animal Acts

There are many possible variations. Typical examples are a lion and a lion trainer or elephant and trainer. The animals are mock-ups with one or two performers inside. The animals can do the opposite of what the trainer says.

Patterns are available for making animal costumes to be worn like a suit. A typical construction of an elephant carried by two performers is shown.

Cloth cover

Basic wire framework
for elephant.

Construction of elephant carried by two performers.

Falling Tables

This act requires considerable skill and practice, but is well worth the effort. Construction details are shown. The tables must be lightweight and sturdy. Special blocks are used to keep the tables from sliding apart and the chair on the top table. This is important. Do not attempt this act without these safety aids.

The clown should learn the basic skills in tumbling before attempting this act. A long tumbling mat is also needed.

Begin practice with one table (the one with the block cutouts for the chair) and the chair. Have a helper to assist. Sit on the chair. Helper then rocks table. When table falls over backwards, clown straddles backwards to feet first landing on the tumbling mat. A backward roll follows the landing.

Try this next with two tables and the chair. The helper stands in front to assist the rocking and to make sure the tables do not fall over forward. The clown should begin at this point to do most of the rocking himself. When the tables fall over backwards, the clown again straddles legs, lands on feet, and does a backward roll.

The final step is with three tables. The helper can assist at first with the rocking. With practice the clown does the entire sequence without help. A number of rocks can be used, as the audience always seems to enjoy the tables when they are almost, but not quite falling. The clown can pretend to be pulling himself back in balance as though there were a rope attached to the wall. The surprise comes when the tables actually topple. The backward roll should be done with sloppy form.

If the clown can also do a good handstand on a chair, the routine can be improved by doing a handstand on the chair on top of the three tables before doing the rocking sequence.

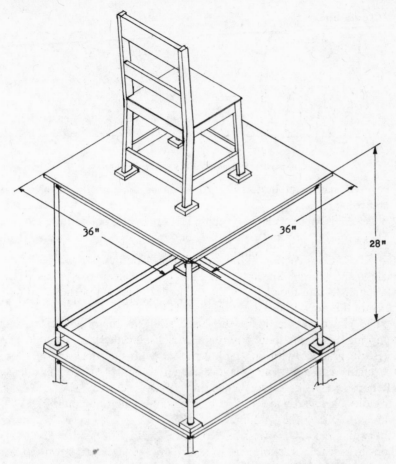

Construction of equipment for falling tables routine.

The rocking part can also be done with the clown pretending to be reading a newspaper, which he is holding in his hands. There can be other clowns on the floor running back and forth as the tables are rocking. They can do this off to the side, pretending that they are shoving the tables back upright.

COSTUMES AND MAKE-UP

Costumes and make-up can add to the effect of clowning. The traditional clown costume is a large, loose-fitting suit. Patterns are available for making these. The material can be any desired color. Candy-striped and polka-dotted patterns are popular. Pom-poms can

Falling tables routine.

be used instead of buttons. Ruffles can be used on the sleeves, legs and collar.

Another popular clown costume is a set of old, poor fitting clothes. These can be torn and patched. A battered hat will add to the effect. Shoes can be painted tennis shoes, or comedy footgear can be constructed.

Make-up can be purchased from theatrical supply shops. Only approved types should be used. The make-up can be applied as

(Courtesy, Warren C. Wood)

Clowns of the 1974 Great Y Circus in Redlands, California.

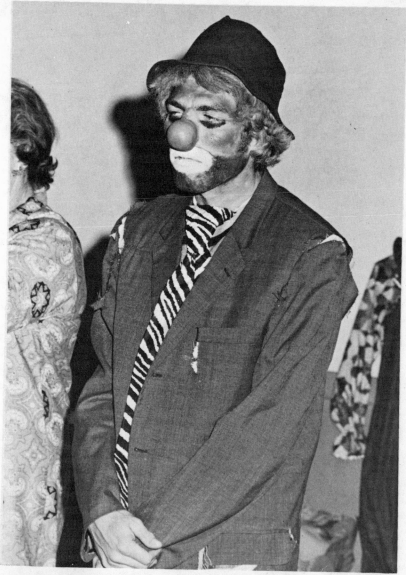

(*Courtesy, Warren C. Wood*)

Clown Ed Smith, formerly with the Great Y Circus in Redlands, California, now a professional with Ringling Blue (Smitty the Clown).

desired. Each clown seems to have his own ideas about this. Other possibilities include masks, special noses and ears, and skull caps.

The costumes and make-up should, of course, fit the style of the particular clown. Some clowns are thin. A fat clown can be made from a thin one by adding pillows under the costumes. Suspenders are another good idea.

THE IMPORTANCE OF ORIGINALITY

Each clown should develop his own style. Creativity is extremely important. Clowning is an art that requires considerable practice, but skilled clowns are an acknowledged asset to an amateur circus.

chapter 21

CIRCUS CLUBS

AND ACTIVITIES

A club can greatly expand the possibilities of circus skills. Through a club interests can be shared, classes held, and activities and amateur circuses sponsored.

THE ADVANTAGES OF CLUBS

In some areas circus clubs are already in operation (see Chapter 2). If there are no suitable clubs in your area, perhaps you can start one. The first step is to locate others who are also interested in circus activities. In some cases this may mean teaching others some of the basic circus skills to create an interested group. One way to do this is to start a circus skills class at a school or community organization.

A small interested group will serve to get things started. Set up a time and place to get together. It's highly recommended that the club be organized through a school or community organization, as this will solve many problems. Advantages include adding prestige to the club, use of facilities and equipment, organizational help, advertising, and promotion. An individual starting a private circus club or school on a commercial basis would immediately run into liability problems. Insurance could be difficult to obtain and costly. It was this factor that put an end to most of the trampoline centers that spread across the country in the late 1950s and early 1960s. Through an organization, the liability and insurance problems are often taken care of.

Volunteer organizations often have a system for starting new clubs. These vary, but generally involve having a certain size group interested in an activity who are members of the organization.

The small organizing group can lay the groundwork for expanding to a regular club. This may take some promoting at first. One way to do this is to demonstrate some circus skills in the community after publishing announcements that a circus club is forming.

At the first regular meeting of the expanded club, matters such as meeting times and places, activities, dues, and so on can be decided. The club can be anything from informal to highly organized. Purposes and goals can be established, officers elected, and committees formed to plan activities.

Generally a valuable asset to circus clubs are skilled circus performers. If there are any in your area, they might be interested in joining the club. Often, once they hear about the club, they will ask if they can join. Most people who are experienced in circus skills enjoy teaching others.

All members of a circus club, however, need not be skilled performers. There's always room for interested beginners and those who are interested in other aspects of amateur circuses, such as building equipment, organizing and promoting, making costumes and props, announcing, and so on and so on.

Circus clubs have been organized for a large age range. Others have been limited to certain age groups. In some cases membership is limited to those who attend a school or college.

A good catchy name can be a great help in promoting a club. Names of successful circus clubs have included the Gymkana and Acro Batos. These may stimulate ideas for a name for your club. In most cases the name should be short and the circus image should be associated with it.

Circus activities are generally so attractive that once a club is started, recruiting new members will not be a problem. Performing in community events and putting on a large annual circus will provide considerable advertisement for the club. After these events a large flux of inquiries generally follow.

CLUB ACTIVITIES

The most successful circus clubs have been those engaged in many activities. This seems to be what people are looking for.

Equipment and Work-Out Areas

A club group can often obtain what an individual alone cannot. There is a heavy demand for the use of most gymnasium facilities. Whereas an individual wouldn't have much chance, an organized group would probably be able to obtain prime use time.

In any case it's important that a circus club have a place for practicing. Indoor facilities are generally best, but when weather permits outdoor areas can be used.

Equipment, especially large and expensive items, is something else that a club is better able to cope with. Many organizations already have some of this. Another possibility is to build equipment. Among the members of most clubs are the resources needed. Someone probably has the skills and equipment needed for welding and so on.

When buying equipment, a club can often get discounts. This is especially helpful in purchasing costumes, shoes, and similar items. If a club is part of a larger organization, it might be possible to purchase through them at wholesale prices.

Thus a club can take advantage of the varied skills of its members and group buying and bargaining power.

Instruction

An ideal club activity is to offer circus skill classes. Beginning classes will offer the skilled members a chance to teach others. Members of these classes will often want to join the club.

Intermediate and advanced classes can also be held if qualified instructors are available. However, even without these the more advanced members can help others improve their skills.

If there are any other circus clubs in the area, exchange get-togethers can be a source of many new ideas and can serve many of the functions of skill classes.

Outings

Circus outings provide fun for all concerned and thus make ideal circus club activities. These can be held at a park. Often they are planned around a picnic. Take along appropriate circus equipment and plan some of the activities around this.

Parade Groups

Many circus clubs perform in parades. Many of the circus skills can be used, such as clowning, bicycling (with special circus bicycle), and unicycling. Apparatus such as trampolines and horizontal bars have been mounted on the backs of trucks for use in parades.

Most parade committees will be happy to have circus activities in the parades. Parades are generally held on holidays, such as the Fourth of July, Veterans' Day, and Memorial Day. Contact the parade committee at least a month ahead of time, as parades are generally organized about this far in advance.

With approval, find out details of parade, including time and meeting place and parade route. Also find out if there are any special rules, such as forward movement only, and plan the demonstration accordingly.

Other points to keep in mind are that parades generally move at slow, erratic paces, with some complete stops. In many cases the parade entries are judged and recognition and awards are given in various categories. Many of the ideas for staging an amateur circus (see next chapter) will also apply to parade routines. A banner can be included with the name of the circus club on it.

Acts and Circuses

Most amateur circus groups perform in community events and for various organizations. In some instances these performances are short, consisting of one or two acts. Sometimes they are complete shows. A circus club should plan various combinations of acts for a variety of situations and performing areas. In some cases only a small stage will be available. In other cases a large area is available. The acts used should be planned accordingly.

A much more ambitious undertaking is a complete amateur circus. These often become annual events, with performances given over two or three day periods. Some amateur circuses also perform on the "road." A few out of town engagements each year greatly add to the fun and experiences of the members of a circus club.

(Courtesy, Dr. Hartley Price)

Doubles act performed by members of the Tallahassee Tumbling Tots.

Planning, organizing, and sponsoring a complete amateur circus can provide a major focus for a club. A variety of talents will be needed, so there's almost certain to be interesting and challenging things for everyone to do. The next chapter gives the information needed for staging and promoting an amateur circus.

chapter 22

ORGANIZING,

PROMOTING,

AND STAGING

AMATEUR CIRCUSES

Throughout this book emphasis has been placed on learning basic circus skills and combining them into acts. These acts form the basis of a complete amateur circus. Organizing, promoting, and staging an amateur circus is the next logical step.

INITIAL STEPS

It generally begins when some person or organization decides that they will have an amateur circus. From the beginning it's probably a good idea to plan the circus through a school, college, or community organization. In most cases the circus will be under the direction of one individual, who will be assisted by a number of others.

In some cases a circus will be sponsored by a community club or organization. Physical education departments often put on amateur circuses. It's best however to avoid sponsors who are interested in promoting or advertising their products.

After a decision has been made to have an amateur circus, a time of year and place should be worked out. Generally this should be

212

done at least six months before the actual circus date. This will give individual acts time to get ready for the big show.

An amateur circus can be put on almost any time of the year, but generally the summer and major holidays should be avoided. Also make sure that the circus will not have to compete with some other event for an audience. Watch especially for dates of large sporting events, as these can drain away a large portion of a potential circus audience.

Amateur circuses are often performed more than once. Typical is one show on a Friday evening and two on Saturday, a matinee and evening performance.

After the dates and times have been decided, a location should be chosen. Basic choices are indoors and outdoors. Indoor locations include gymnasiums and auditoriums. Outdoor performances can be given in stadiums and other places where appropriate seating can be set up or is already in place.

For a newly formed amateur circus, an overly large seating area will not be necessary. This will vary depending on many factors, but successful amateur circuses have been held with seating for audiences of less than five hundred. The fame of an amateur circus will generally grow from year to year, and the locations can be changed accordingly.

If the organization giving the circus has its own facilities for holding the event, many problems are automatically solved. If not, try to find a place that can be used free or, at most, for a very nominal fee.

Other early considerations are whether or not admission will be charged and, if so, where the money will go. In many cases amateur circuses are used as annual fund raising events. There may be ordinances involved, so check this out.

Decisions should be made concerning advanced ticket sales, such as how many and when they will go on sale. This is typically done months before the actual circus date, even though the tickets probably won't go on sale until about a month before the show.

The advertising should also be planned far ahead of time. By this point committees should be formed to handle various aspects of the circus. Methods of advertising include posters, newspapers, television, and radio.

Posters should include the name of the circus, the sponsoring school or organization, the day, date, and time, and the admission price. If appropriate, also include information about advance ticket sales. It can also be helpful to state where the money is to go and how it is to be used. However, keep the posters as brief and to the point as possible. Posters can be printed by hand, but professional printing is generally a better idea. There are many printing shops that can now do this quickly and at low cost. Some of the methods can reproduce photographs on the posters.

Other things that must be taken care of before the circus performances are making up the program and having copies made and getting the tickets printed.

ORGANIZING AND STAGING

After individual acts have been worked up as detailed in this book, there's still a lot of work to do to organize and stage this into a complete amateur circus.

Program

The individual acts should be arranged into a program. Here are some suggestions:

1. The entire show should be about ninety minutes, including an intermission.

2. About a dozen main acts seems to work out well.

3. The intermission should be one or two acts past thè half-way point in the show.

4. Solo acts should be limited to about six minutes duration. Group acts should be twelve minutes or less in most cases. Every act should be as short as possible.

5. Begin with grand entry parade. Some amateur circuses also end with a short parade or other arrangement to give everyone a chance to take a bow.

6. Get the audience's attention immediately. Hold it by generating excitement. Taper off a little, then arrange acts to build to center act. After intermission, start show with bang again. Taper off somewhat, then build to most spectacular peak—the finale.

7. When arranging acts, use variety and contrast to sustain audience interest.

8. Be sure to consider setting up and taking down equipment in placement of acts.

9. Comedy should be mixed into the show at appropriate times.

10. A smooth dovetailing of acts is important.

Before the actual show, printed programs should be made up for the audience.

The Acts

Each act should be as polished as possible. The acts must not drag. They should be short, snappy, and to the point. The general rule is to finish each act with the audience wanting more.

Styling of each act is important. Work on the timing, pacing, and taking bows. Watch professional circus performers for ideas on styling.

Choose a catchy name for each act. In most cases this should be one or two words.

Entrances and exits should be practiced. Performers should learn to spot each other. Placement and movement of equipment and props should be carefully planned.

For each act the lighting, music, and script should be worked out. The script will be used by the master of ceremonies to introduce the act and make commentaries.

Each act should be worked out so that the time it takes is known. This will help greatly in putting a complete program together.

Costumes can add to the effect. Choose ones that are appropriate for the type of act being presented. The costumes need not be expensive. In many cases standard gymnastic pants and shirts have been used by male performers, and leotards by the girls. Various types of pants and shirts can also be used. A bright colored sash tied about the waist will add a circus flavor.

Costumes can also be sewn from patterns. This method is commonly used by the more established amateur circuses. Often there is a committee that sees to this.

While in general each act can select the costumes to be used, it's important that there be enough variety between acts so that they don't look like the same performers. Also, if the same performers are in more than one act, it's a good idea if different uniforms are worn for each one.

Here are some other suggestions for the individual acts:

1. Keep it simple and neat.
2. Use only those tricks that can be done well. A missed stunt can be used to build suspense, but this should be on purpose, not an accident.
3. The act should have variety and contrast and lead to a climax.
4. Be creative and artistic.
5. Be in control of the act.

Costumes worn by a baton act in the Great Y Circus in Redlands, California.

6. Each performer must know exactly what to do at all times. The time between tricks is extremely important.

7. Try to introduce the element of surprise.

8. Practice the act the way it will be done in the actual show over and over again. If this is not done, the audience will almost always know it.

Organizing

In most cases there will be a circus director, who will need a number of assistants. The assistants can be in charge of various phases of the show, such as clowns, regular acts, grand entry parade, music, and equipment and props.

Start working up a continuity sheet several weeks before the actual show. This should include the running time of the show, length and starting time of each act, costumes to be used, and lights, script, and music required. This should be fairly well worked out before the rehearsals of the complete show. Some modifications may be made at rehearsals, but these should be kept to a minimum.

(Courtesy, Warren C. Wood)

Practice session for a unicycle act in the Great Y Circus.

Master of Ceremonies

This is an important part of an amateur circus. Choose this person carefully. A script should be used and followed closely, yet the master of ceremonies must be able to *ad lib* in case of unforeseen delays.

The master of ceremonies should be selected early and have a part in working up the script. A decision needs to be made as to whether or not to announce the names of performers. With children the names should be given if at all possible. In acts with very large numbers of performers, the names can be given as a stunt is performed. If it seems impractical to give the names during the acts, they can be given during the grand entry parade. Another possibility is to include the names in the printed program and just announce the names of the acts during the show.

In most cases it's best to keep running commentaries to a minimum during acts. Unusual or interesting stunts can be explained, but this should not be overdone. Let the acts speak for themselves whenever possible. In some cases an announcement may be part of the act. Comedy frequently makes use of this. The master of ceremonies may, for example, ask for a volunteer from the audience. This is frequently done when a performer has been "planted" in the audience.

Grand Entry and Exit Parades

A grand entry parade makes an excellent way to start the show. Generally all performers participate. If the show is in a gymnasium, the pattern can be from the performers' entrance-exit, around the gym, and out again. The performers can be in regular or special costumes. Special props, such as animals with one or two people inside, can be used. Clowns can be on stilts. The parade can be led by a person carrying a flag. The parade should be colorful. Flags, streamers, and pennants can add to the effect. Music should accompany the parade.

Novelty items are ideal for grand entry parades. Unusual cycles and carts can be used. Various types of floats on wheels that are pulled along are another idea.

The grand entry parade will take only about four or five minutes, yet it will start the show off with a promise that more is to come.

Music and Lighting

If possible, band music should be used. School bands will often provide this. They should attend the rehearsals. Record or tape music is a possibility if nothing in the way of live music is available.

The use of lighting should be carefully planned. Most auditoriums and multi-purpose gymnasiums are equipped to provide special lighting. In many cases experienced help is available for operating this equipment. Spotlights should be used with discretion, as they can hinder the performance of some stunts.

If special lighting is not available, the show can still be successful. If considered as essential, spotlights can be rented.

Equipment and Props

The equipment and props used in the various acts must be arranged and stored so that the items needed are ready to go. In some cases there will be stage hands to move and set up equipment, in other cases the performers themselves will do it.

Equipment and props can be a major problem if the show is performed in a place where the equipment cannot be brought in until the day of the show. This will take special planning.

Equipment used in some acts may require special rigging. In some situations it will be impractical to use some of the acts. The program can be adjusted accordingly.

Equipment and props should be handled smoothly, with as little noise and confusion as possible. Dimming lights can help here.

A continuity sheet should be worked out for the handling of equipment and props. The sheet should be posted in a convenient location for constant checking. Many acts have been spoiled by not having a piece of equipment when needed.

Some items used in individual acts can be the responsibility of the performers themselves. A juggling act, for example, should have balls, rings, clubs, and other equipment organized for the act. A good way to do this is to have a cart or basket with everything arranged in the order that it will be needed. A check sheet can save embarrassment.

Backstage

The performers should be quiet at all times, as noise will quickly reach the level where it can be heard by the audience. The acts should be called ahead of time. A five-minute-before-act call can be used. The act should be ready to go when the announcement is made by the master of ceremonies.

Dressing rooms will also have to be organized. Costumes can be arranged on racks. Pins and sewing equipment should be ready for emergency repair of costumes.

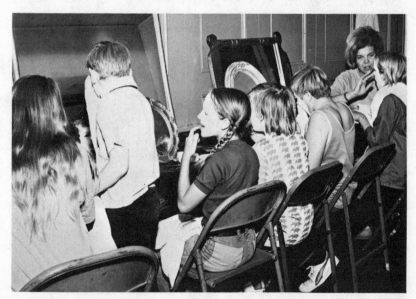

(Courtesy, Warren C. Wood)

Backstage—clowns in the Great Y Circus applying make-up.

Rehearsals

At least one full-dress rehearsal should be held. This is generally done a few days before the actual show. This should be, if possible, just the way the show will be performed before the audience, including costumes, music, lighting, and announcing. All acts should be performed just as they will be done in the show.

Some acts will probably want to "walk through." Try to avoid this. Acts that cannot be done in practice are generally too difficult to use in a show.

In addition to the full-dress rehearsal, two or three walk-through practices should be held. For these, it's a good idea to set up all equipment and move all props as they will be needed. In many cases this will be the first time everyone is together. Final problems can be ironed out.

In the final full-dress rehearsal, changes or additions should be avoided unless absolutely necessary. Many an amateur circus director has aged ten years on this day! It's seldom possible to get any life into the show without an audience. Don't worry too much about this, however. The thing is to get through the entire show.

POINTERS RE THE ACTUAL SHOW

With the audience there are additional considerations. Tickets must be collected. Programs are generally passed out. In most cases refreshments will be sold. If reserved seating is used, ushers must be available to help in the seating.

Often walkaround clowns are used before the show to keep the audience amused while they are waiting.

The show should start right on time. The intermission should be announced so that the audience will know when the second half of the show is to begin. The second half should begin right on time. Wrap up the show in a grand manner and on time. A ninety minute show should be over in ninety minutes.

In most cases the performers outdo themselves before the live audience. There are bound to be a few mistakes. Soothe hurt feelings. An amateur circus should be fun for everyone, including performers.

ABOUT SPECIAL PERFORMANCES

Besides annual circuses, many groups also do special performances. In some cases these performances have been out of town, adding a travel experience. A few amateur circuses have traveled to other countries.

Once the reputation of an amateur circus reaches a high level, there's seldom a problem in getting shows. The difficulty will most likely be in selecting which ones.

It may be necessary to modify the show for special performances. It's a good idea to have versions worked out for gyms, auditoriums, and outdoor areas.

(Photo by Bob Lynn)

Danny Haynes of the Hamilton Mini Circus riding a unicycle across high wire.